Wildflowers
OF WYOMING

Diantha States
and
Jack States

2004
MOUNTAIN PRESS PUBLISHING COMPANY
Missoula, Montana

Cover design by Kim Ericsson based on the authors' photograph of scarlet Indian paintbrush *(Castilleja miniata)*

Library of Congress Cataloging-in-Publication Data
States, Diantha, 1941-
    Wildflowers of Wyoming / Diantha States and Jack States.
        p. cm.
    ISBN 0-87842-496-2 (pbk. : alk. paper)
    1. Wild flowers–Wyoming–Identification. 2. Wild flowers–Wyoming–
    Pictorial works. I. States, Jack S., 1941- II. Title.
        QK195.S725 2004
        582.13'09787–dc22

                                                              2003023545

PRINTED IN HONG KONG BY MANTEC PRODUCTION COMPANY

Mountain Press Publishing Company
P.O. Box 2399 • Missoula, Montana 59806
(406) 728-1900

We dedicate this book to our mothers,

Jean and Guen,

who share our joy and interest

in the wonders of wildflowers.

CONTENTS

ACKNOWLEDGMENTS

We wish to thank everyone who offered us encouragement and friendship while we were writing this book. LaRea Dennis Johnston, Nancy and Ellery Worthen, and Martha Christensen graciously contributed floras from surrounding areas. David and Micki Schuster and Sid and Lois Trouwborst allowed us to photograph wildflowers growing on their land. Ken and Jeanine Green, Alyce Jolovich, Bob and Barb Spengler, and Jim and Jeffrey States accompanied us on hikes to locate and photograph wildflowers. Dorothy Tuthill reviewed the photos and helped us with common names. Our heartfelt thanks to Janel States James for reading the manuscript and to Dr. Richard Scott for providing a technical review and many helpful suggestions. Dr. Ron Hartman and the Rocky Mountain Herbarium provided us plant identification assistance.

INTRODUCTION

Wyoming is home to a host of spectacular wildflowers. From the plains to the high mountains a kaleidoscope of flowers abound. This field guide presents a unique overview of the native wildflowers and flowering shrubs that you are likely to encounter throughout the growing season in Wyoming. We had two goals in writing this book. The first was to provide readers unfamiliar with plant identification an easy-to-use field guide; the second goal was to write a book that included the common wildflowers of the six major vegetation zones in Wyoming: alpine, subalpine, montane, steppe, foothills, and plains. And, for the first time, it will be possible for plant enthusiasts to identify and enjoy Wyoming wildflowers using only one field guide.

We provided color photographs of each plant in its natural setting along with descriptions of wildflowers representing 54 plant families, 218 genera, and over 325 species. We excluded introduced plants even though some are quite common and showy. Descriptions and photographs of introduced plants can be found in *Weeds of the West* (Whitson, 1992).

We described plants with a minimum of technical terms and provided line drawings of leaves and flowers to define the technical terms we have used. The plant descriptions include notes on habitat and ecology, geographic distribution, and information about related species. In some cases we noted native uses of plants and the origin of common and scientific names.

Many Wyoming wildflowers also inhabit similar vegetation zones of adjoining states as shown on the map on page 3. This guide will also be useful to identify wildflowers in western Nebraska, western South Dakota, southern Montana, eastern Idaho, northeastern Utah, and northern Colorado. Much of this region of the Rocky Mountain West falls in four national parks, four national grasslands, three national monuments, eleven national forests, and vast tracts of Bureau of Land Management land. These readily accessible public lands are wonderful places to observe and enjoy wildflowers. Even though many of the plants included in this guide have a broad distribution throughout the western United States, we have focused on the most common, showy wildflowers found in Wyoming.

LANDSCAPE, CLIMATE, AND WILDFLOWER DIVERSITY

Wyoming occupies a unique geographic position in North America. Its midcontinental location, northerly latitude, and average elevation of 6,700 feet gives it a dry, cold, and temperate climate characterized by dramatic seasonal changes. Elevations range from 3,100 feet in northeastern Wyoming to 13,804 feet at Gannett Peak in the Wind River Range. Most precipitation falls as snow in winter and early spring with limited rainfall falling midsummer. Annual precipitation ranges from an average 10 to 20 inches in the eastern plains, less than 10 inches in some locations of the sagebrush steppe, to as much as 60 inches in the western mountains.

The mountainous Continental Divide runs southeast to northwest through the state, physically separating eastern Wyoming's short-grass prairie, an extension of the eastern Great Plains flora, from western Wyoming's sagebrush steppe, the eastern extension of the Great Basin flora. In Wyoming the floras of the northern and southern branches of the Rocky Mountains merge in the central Rockies, and a number of wildflowers reach the southern and northern extent of their range.

The remarkable diversity of flowering plant species in Wyoming is due, in part, to the adaptations of plants to Wyoming's great variety of habitats and highly variable climate. Wyoming's wildflower diversity can also be attributed to extensive floral invasions of the geologic past. As the continental glaciers melted and retreated thousands of years ago, and suitable habitats became available, a diverse cadre of plants followed the drainages of the West's major river systems—the Missouri, Colorado, and Columbia—to their headwaters in the snow-capped mountains of Wyoming. This migration resulted in a grand convergence of floral representatives from the eastern Great Plains, the desert Southwest, and the Pacific Northwest.

VEGETATION ZONES

Vegetation–especially vegetation in the western United States–is distributed in distinctive bands, or zones, that are composed of plants that tolerate similar ecological conditions. This zonation is caused by differences in average annual temperature and precipitation, both of which change with elevation and latitude. If you were to travel north, the average annual temperature decreases about one degree Fahrenheit for each degree of latitude; there is a corresponding decrease of about one degree Fahrenheit for each 250 to 330 feet increase in elevation. Precipitation increases at the rate of 4 to 5 inches for every 1,000 feet of additional elevation.

Sometimes called "life" zones by ecologists, vegetation zones are natural associations of characteristic plant species adapted to the specific temperature and precipitation conditions of each zone.

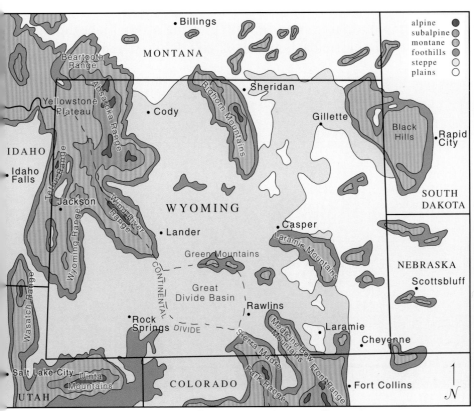

Vegetation zones of Wyoming and surrounding region

Perennial herbs and low-growing shrubs characterize the alpine zone, while trees, shrubs, and perennial grasses are the most prevalent plant types found in the subalpine, montane, foothills, steppe, and plains zones. In addition to elevation and latitude, the boundaries of these zones are collectively influenced by northern and southern slope exposure, rain-shadow effect on the leeward sides of mountain ranges, and soil conditions.

Alpine

The alpine (tundra) zone begins above timberline at about 9,800 feet and higher. Devoid of trees, the alpine zone is populated with a variety of perennial herbs and dwarf shrubs that form compact cushions or dense mats to minimize their exposure to wind, extreme cold, and drought. The treeless mountaintops are home to a variety of wildflowers that often bloom at the same time resulting in a breathtaking display of color across the alpine meadows. They flower rapidly to maximize the short growing season (June through August). Unforgettable bouquets of colorful moss campion *(Silene*

**The alpine zone (above the spruce-fir forest)
in the Teton Range, Wyoming**

**Subalpine spruce-fir forest and open meadows
in the Wind River Range, Wyoming**

acaulis), old man of the mountain *(Hymenoxys grandiflora)*, alpine forget-me-not *(Eritrichum nanum)*, sky pilot *(Polemonium viscosum)*, and alpine avens *(Geum rossii)* highlight midsummer hikes through this zone.

Subalpine

The subalpine zone, 9,000 to 9,800 feet, has broad, open meadows (often called "parks") interspersed in a conifer forest. The forest is dominated by Engelmann spruce *(Picea engelmannii)* and subalpine fir *(Abies* species). In some areas lodgepole pine *(Pinus contorta)* and aspen *(Populus tremuloides)* are mixed with the spruce and fir. In the western mountain ranges, western whitebark pine *(Pinus albicaulis)* replaces spruce and subalpine fir near timberline. Timberline defines the border between the subalpine forest and the treeless alpine zone. Common wildflowers in this zone are Indian paintbrush *(Castilleja* species), arnica *(Arnica* species), lousewort *(Pedicularis* species), columbine *(Aquilegia* species), American bistort *(Polygonum bistortoides)*, and streamside bluebells *(Mertensia ciliata)*. Expect these flowers to be at their peak bloom in July.

Montane forest and meadows in the Bighorn Range, Wyoming

Montane

Wide expanses of pine and aspen characterize the montane zone, which lies between 6,800 and 9,000 feet. Three dominant species of pine are found in this zone. Ponderosa pine *(Pinus ponderosa)* occurs in the Black Hills of eastern Wyoming and western South Dakota, the eastern slopes of the Bighorn Range, the Laramie Mountains, and the eastern slopes of the Colorado Front Range. In the central and western mountains of Wyoming limber pine *(Pinus flexilis)* occurs at lower elevations and lodgepole pine is widespread at higher elevations. Aspen is found in wetter soils, often on north-facing slopes. Open slopes and meadows break the expanse of forest in the montane zone. The greatest diversity of mountain wildflowers in the montane zone occurs where streams meander through these sunny openings. Look for wild buckwheat (*Eriogonum* species), monkshood (*Aconitum columbianum*), fireweed (*Chamerion* species), lupine (*Lupinus* species), and nodding little sunflower *(Helianthella quinquenervis)* from June into August.

Foothills

The foothills zone marks the transition from grass-dominated plains in eastern Wyoming and sagebrush steppe in central and western Wyoming to the montane zone. The vegetation here is a mosaic of grasses, shrubs, and conifer woodland (a forest with an open canopy). The dominant trees are Utah juniper *(Juniperus osteosperma)* and Rocky Mountain juniper *(Juniperus scopularum)* at elevations of 3,600 to 6,300 feet while combinations of ponderosa pine, limber pine, and Douglas fir *(Pseudotsuga menziesii)* are prevalent at 5,400 to 8,000 feet. Various flowering shrubs can be found in treeless areas and under the open tree canopies. These include Wyoming big sagebrush *(Artemisia tridentata)*, mountain mahogany *(Cercocarpus* species), serviceberry *(Amelanchier* species), antelope bitterbrush *(Purshia tridentata)*, skunkbush sumac *(Rhus aromatica)*, snowbrush *(Ceanothus* species), and dogbane *(Apocynum* species). The deciduous aspen extends from its usual range in the montane zone down into the foothills zone along moist drainages. Conversely, cottonwood

Foothills, where plains and steppe meet the montane zone, at Elk Mountain, Wyoming

Sagebrush steppe on Beaver Rim in central Wyoming

(*Populus* species), a plains inhabitant, follows the drainages upwards into the foothills and montane zones. Common foothills wildflowers include blanketflower *(Gaillardia aristata),* balsamroot (*Balsamorhiza* species), lupine (*Lupinus* species), flax (*Linum* species), and skyrocket *(Ipomopsis aggregata).*

Steppe

Stretching west of the Great Plains to Nevada and Oregon is a wide expanse of steppe ranging from 3,100 to 6,500 feet. It is dominated by the perennial shrubs Wyoming big sagebrush, greasewood *(Sarcobatus vermiculatus),* shadscale *(Atriplex confertifolia),* and four-winged saltbush *(Atriplex canescens).* In Wyoming sagebrush blankets broad areas between the mountain ranges and escarpments (uplifts) on the western side of the Continental Divide, while plains vegetation and sagebrush steppe often occur at the same elevation on the eastern side. This distribution is primarily governed by average annual precipitation. For example, short-grass prairie occurs on the Laramie Plains, a high-elevation (7,000 feet) area where one might expect to see sagebrush, partially because more summer precipitation falls there. Wildflowers bloom in the steppe early in the season to take advantage of spring moisture before the dry, hot summer. Expect to find phlox (*Phlox* species), Indian paintbrush *(Castilleja* species), larkspur (*Delphinium* species), locoweed (*Oxytropis* species), shooting star (*Dodecatheon* species), and sego lily *(Calochortus nuttallii)* blooming during May and June.

Plains

The plains zone, located at the western extent of the North American Great Plains, generally occurs at 3,100 to 6,500 feet. Mixed- and short-grass prairies are dominated by the perennial grasses buffalo grass *(Buchloë dachtyloides),* blue grass (*Poa* species), needle-and-thread grass *(Heterostipa comata)* and blue grama *(Bouteloua gracilis).* The deciduous trees cottonwood, green ash *(Fraxinus pennsylvanica),* and box elder *(Acer negundo)* grow along watercourses. Here, precipitation comes as winter snow and summer thunderstorms. Some common flowers associated with this zone are pasqueflower *(Anemone patens),* milkvetch (*Astragalus* species), beardtongue (*Penstemon* species), coneflower (*Ratibida* species), and dotted gayfeather *(Liatris punctata).*

Plains in eastern Wyoming and western South Dakota

How To Use This Book

There are far too many species of wildflowers in Wyoming for us to have included them all in this field guide. We have described plants of the most common and showy genera. Although many published field guides are organized by flower color, we have followed the accepted botanical practice of arranging wildflowers by plant family. This approach groups them in a natural classification based on floral form (morphology). Families appear in alphabetical order by common name, while genera within the families are in alphabetical order.

To help identify the various plants we purposely selected plant characteristics that can be seen without magnification. Botanical terms used to describe leaves and flowers are illustrated with line drawings and can be found inside the back cover. On pages 17–18 we included line drawings of sixteen of the largest families we presented in the book. These illustrations include a sketch of general plant and flower shape with notes of family characteristics.

We included two sections to help amateur botanists identify plants. The Key to Plant Families will direct you to the family section where you may find a match for an unknown flower. We provided photo thumbnails of representative herbaceous wildflowers and flowering shrubs, grouped by color and flower shape, for those who find photographs useful to identify plants.

Each wildflower is identified by the common name most frequently used in Wyoming and by its scientific name. A scientific name is composed of two words, the genus and the species. The scientific names are written in Latin and may be derived from Greek or Latin words. Often names honor a person, reflect a geographic location, or describe a plant's characteristics. For example, Wyoming Indian paintbrush is named *Castilleja linariifolia*. The genus *Castilleja* was given in honor of a Spanish botanist, Domingo Castillejo (1744–1793). The species name *linariifolia* means "narrow leaves" and describes the leaves that are typical of this wildflower.

Some scientific names have been changed recently, especially in the sunflower family. We used the new names but have noted the old, familiar ones as well. In addition, some botanists have reclassified genera in several families, most notably the lily family (Liliaceae), and have placed them in several new families. We retained the familiar lily family association while noting the new family designations in the plant descriptions. The scientific names are current with Dorn's *Vascular Plants of Wyoming* (2001).

Descriptions include general plant characteristics with size, leaf form and arrangement, and flower form and arrangement. The measurements and bloom times we give are averages. We have also indicated the number of species that occur within each genus in Wyoming and the habitat, life zone, and distribution of each species. Many wildlfowers grow in quite specific habitats and the descriptions indicate any unusual or specific habitat requirements. Although many of the wildflowers are widely distributed, we have limited our discussion of their distribution to western North America, west of the hundredth meridian in the central Great Plains (Manitoba south to Texas) to the Cascade Range of western British Columbia, Washington, Oregon, and California.

For general interest, we have included some notes on edibility and medicinal uses. We do not recommend using or consuming any of the wildflowers. Neither the authors nor the publisher accepts responsibility for the reader's identification or the consequences of eating or using any of the wildflowers listed in this book.

Many parks and forests have rules prohibiting wildflower picking. It goes without saying that wildflowers should not be picked or disturbed. Develop the habit of observation, take photographs or make sketches, and leave the flowers for others to enjoy.

For further study, we have included a list of useful references for plants of the area, as well as plant societies. For those wishing to keep a "life list" of wildflowers, we provided check boxes in the index.

CHARACTERISTICS OF SIXTEEN SELECTED FAMILIES

borage family pp. 30–37

• regular flowers have five united petals and sometimes occur in coiled clusters

• simple, alternate leaves are often hairy and sticky

buckwheat family pp. 38–43

• small flowers have four, five, or six papery petal-like sepals, no petals, and occur in rounded clusters

• simple leaves are basal or alternate

buttercup family pp. 44–57

• flowers can be regular or irregular, have five or more petals (or no petals), five sepals or petal-like sepals, and many stamens; sepals and petals may have hoods or spurs

• leaves are simple or compound

carrot family pp. 62–67

• small, regular flowers have five petals and are usually grouped in rounded clusters

• compound leaves are alternate or basal and often finely divided

figwort family pp. 76–89

• irregular flowers have five united petals

• leaves are opposite or alternate

gentian family pp. 94–97

• flowers have four or five united petals

• leaves are opposite or whorled

heath family pp. 100–7

• urn- or saucer-shaped flowers have five united petals

• evergreen leaves are usually basal

lily family pp. 114–23

• flowers have three petals and three sepals or petal-like sepals

• simple leaves have parallel veins and are alternate or basal

CHARACTERISTICS OF SIXTEEN SELECTED FAMILIES

mint family pp. 130–33

• flowers are irregular and have five petals united into two lips
• stem is square in cross section
• leaves are simple, opposite, and toothed
• plants are often aromatic

mustard family pp. 134–41

• flowers have four separate petals and six stamens
• fruits form below flowers on flower stalk
• leaves are alternate and simple or compound

orchid family pp. 142–45

• flowers have three petal-like sepals and three petals; the lower petal is inflated into a lip
• the simple leaves are alternate or basal and have parallel veins

pea family pp. 146–59

• flowers are irregular and have five united petals and ten partly united stamens; petals are modified into two wings, a banner, and a keel

• leaves are pinnately or palmately compound, and alternate or basal

phlox family pp. 160–62

• flowers have five petals united into a tube with flaring tips

• stigma has three lobes

• simple leaves are alternate

rose family pp. 172–85

• flowers have five separate petals and ten stamens

• leaves are simple or compound, usually toothed, and have stipules at the base

saxifrage family pp. 188–93

• flowers have five petals and are clustered along upright stalks

• basal leaves are simple and usually palmately veined

sunflower family pp. 198–238

• flower heads are clusters of petal-like ray flowers and tubular disk flowers; some heads have only ray flowers or only disk flowers

• leaves are alternate, opposite, or basal

KEY TO PLANT FAMILIES

This key will help you determine what family a plant you want to identify belongs to. To use it, start at the beginning of the key and work your way down. Be sure to read all the choices (a, b, c, d, e) for each number before moving further down the key. Once you have found a possible family match, go to that section of the book to identify the plant you have in front of you. Keep in mind that individual families may appear in several places in the key. If you cannot find the plant, try the key again. Also, you might find the line drawings that follow this key useful to identify families. Using keys can be frustrating, but success comes with patience and experience.

1a.	Aquatic plants with stems and leaves wholly or partly submerged	2
1b.	Terrestrial plants growing on land, some in wet places	5
2a.	Tiny flowers or flowers with indistinguishable parts grouped in round or erect clusters	3
2b.	Flowers with colored sepals or petals	4
3a.	Pink flowers in compact, erect clusters; oval, reddish green leaves	**Buckwheat Family p. 38**
3b.	Whitish to greenish flowers in a round cluster; grasslike leaves	**Bur-Reed Family p. 42**
3c.	Greenish to brown flowers in dense, cylindrical clusters; tall leaves	**Cattail Family p. 66**
3d.	Whitish flowers in small clusters at intervals along a stalk; narrow leaves	**Water Milfoil Family p. 244**
4a.	Yellow flowers with large, waxy sepals; leaves simple, very large, floating	**Water-Lily Family p. 244**
4b.	White flowers with five fringed petals; compound leaves with three leaflets	**Buckbean Family p. 36**
4c.	White or yellow flowers with five petals and many stamens; compound leaves	**Buttercup Family p. 44**
4d.	White flowers with three petals; simple, arrowhead-shaped leaves	**Water-Plantain Family p. 244**
5a.	Plants that are not green (lack chlorophyll)	6
5b.	Plants that are green (have chlorophyll)	7
6a.	Pinkish, dull orange, to brownish flowers with five petals	**Heath Family p. 100**
6b.	Reddish flowers with three petal-like sepals and three petals; one petal is a saclike lower lip	**Orchid Family p. 142**

18a. Opposite leaves with coarsely toothed margins;
　　　stem square in cross section .... **Mint Family p. 130**

18b. Opposite or alternate leaves; stem round in cross section; flowers in open clusters
　　　(some enclosed by colored leafy bracts) .... **Figwort Family p. 76**

19a. Opposite leaves 20

19b. Alternate or basal leaves 21

20a. Flowers in flat-topped clusters .... **Valerian Family p. 238**

20b. Flowers in erect clusters and enclosed by colored,
　　　leafy bracts .... **Figwort Family p. 76**

21a. Flowers in erect clusters with five petals united in two lips or in small tubular
　　　flowers enclosed by colored leafy bracts .... **Figwort Family p. 76**

21b. Flowers with four united petals that are
　　　spurred or curved .... **Fumitory Family p. 92**

21c. Flowers with five petals that form a banner, wings,
　　　and a keel .... **Pea Family p. 146**

22a. Small, inconspicuous flowers without petals 23

22b. Showy flowers with petals or petal-like sepals 24

23a. Whitish or greenish flowers; compound or
　　　divided leaves .... **Buttercup Family p. 44**

23b. Greenish flowers; simple leaves with stinging hair .... **Nettle Family p. 140**

23c. Flowers with purplish stamens; toothed leaves .... **Figwort Family p. 76**

24a. More than ten stamens 25

24b. Ten or less stamens 32

25a. One pistil (styles may be divided) 26

25b. Usually more than one pistil 29

26a. Leaves not present; stems fleshy with spines .... **Cactus Family p. 58**

26b. Prickly leaves 27

26c. Leaves not prickly 28

27a. Flowers with five or eight to ten petals; five sepals;
　　　clear juice .... **Stickleaf Family p. 192**

27b. Flowers with six petals; two sepals; milky juice .... **Poppy Family p. 166**

28a. Flowers with five petals; stamens united into a column;
　　　palmately divided, alternate leaves .... **Mallow Family p. 124**

28b. Flowers with five petals; protruding stamens;
　　　simple, opposite leaves .... **St. John's Wort Family p. 186**

28c. Flowers with five to eighteen petals;
　　　fleshy, alternate or basal leaves .... **Purslane Family p. 170**

29a. Simple leaves 30

29b. Compound or deeply divided leaves 31

PHOTO THUMBNAILS

To help readers identify Wyoming's most common wildflowers without using the key, we included photo thumbnails of them arranged by color and shape. We separated the wildflowers into five color groups: white to cream, yellow to gold, pink and red to reddish brown, blue to purple, and green, plus a separate category for flowering shrubs. Since each of us perceives color differently and because individual species can be many different shades of a particular color, you may need to look at flowers in closely related color categories for a match.

Within each color group we further separated the wildflowers by flower shape: flowers with separate petals; flowers with united petals; flower heads of ray flowers and disk flowers; flowers in erect clusters; flowers in rounded clusters.

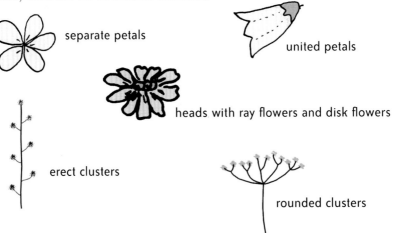

separate petals

united petals

heads with ray flowers and disk flowers

erect clusters

rounded clusters

Symbols used with Photo Thumbnails

WHITE flowers with separate petals

pp. 36–37 pp. 50–51 pp. 50–51 pp. 56–57

pp. 70–71 pp. 74–75 pp. 98–99 pp. 102–3 pp. 116–17

pp. 164–65 pp. 166–67 pp. 174–75 pp. 188–89 pp. 190–91

pp. 192–93 pp. 240–41 pp. 244–45

WHITE flowers with united petals

pp. 120–21

pp. 160–61

WHITE flower heads with ray and disk flowers

pp. 198–99 pp. 200–1 pp. 200–1

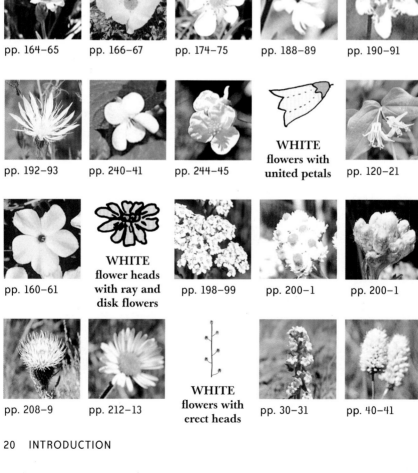

pp. 208–9 pp. 212–13

WHITE flowers with erect heads

pp. 30–31 pp. 40–41

pp. 44–45 pp. 84–85 pp. 104–5 pp. 120–21 pp. 122–23

pp. 122–23 pp. 124–25 pp. 144–45 pp. 148–49 pp. 190–91

WHITE
flowers in
round clusters pp. 62–63 pp. 114–15 pp. 124–25 pp. 134–35

pp. 136–37 pp. 154–55 pp. 164–65 pp. 186–87 **YELLOW**
flowers with
separate petals

pp. 54–55 pp. 58–59 pp. 74–75 pp. 82–83 pp. 116–17

pp. 136–37 pp. 178–79 pp. 182–83 pp. 186–87 pp. 240–41

YELLOW flowers with united petals pp. 32–33

pp. 118–19

YELLOW flower heads with ray and disk flowers

pp. 198–99

pp. 202–3

pp. 220–21

pp. 222–23

pp. 228–29

pp. 230–31

YELLOW flowers with erect heads pp. 78–79

pp. 84–85

pp. 92–93

pp. 136–37

pp. 156–57

pp. 232–33

YELLOW flowers in round clusters pp. 38–39

pp. 64–65

pp. 194–95

BLUE flowers with separate petals pp. 32–33

pp. 46–47

pp. 48–49

pp. 50–51

pp. 90–91

pp. 96–97

pp. 112–13

pp. 112–13

BLUE
flowers with
united petals

pp. 28–29

pp. 94–95

BLUE
flower heads
with ray and
disk flowers

pp. 226–27

BLUE
flowers with
erect heads

pp. 34–35

pp. 44–45

pp. 52–53

pp. 86–87

pp. 152–53

pp. 162–63

pp. 242–43

RED
flowers with
separate petals

pp. 46–47

pp. 48–49

pp. 72–73

pp. 82–83

pp. 98–99

pp. 100–1

pp. 102–3

pp. 126–27

pp. 126–27

pp. 158–59

pp. 166–67

pp. 168–69

pp. 168–69

pp. 170–71

pp. 170–71

RED
flowers with
united petals

pp. 92–93

pp. 106–7

pp. 116–17

pp. 142–43

pp. 160–61

pp. 160–61

pp. 174–75

RED
flower heads
with ray and
disk flowers

pp. 210–11

pp. 226–27

pp. 234–35

RED
flowers with
erect heads

pp. 42–43

pp. 60–61

pp. 76–77

pp. 84–85

pp. 100–1

pp. 104–5

pp. 104–5

pp. 132–33

pp. 142–43

pp. 150–51

RED
flowers in
round clusters

pp. 38–39

pp. 40–41

pp. 70–71

pp. 114–15

pp. 128–29

pp. 132–33

pp. 152–53

pp. 158–59

pp. 194–95

pp. 224–25

GREEN
flowers with
separate petals

pp. 94–95

GREEN
flowers with
united petals

pp. 94–95

GREEN
flower heads
with ray and
disk flowers

pp. 204–5

pp. 208–9

**FLOWERING
SHRUBS**

pp. 26–27

pp. 36–37

pp. 68–69

pp. 68–69

pp. 70–71

pp. 100–1

pp. 108–9

pp. 110–11

pp. 110–11

pp. 172–73

pp. 172–73

pp. 176–77

pp. 180–81

pp. 180–81

pp. 180–81

pp. 184–85

pp. 184–85

pp. 204–5

pp. 212–13

WILDFLOWERS

AGAVE FAMILY   Agavaceae

The agave family is composed of perennials with long-lived, succulent leaves. Arranged on tall stalks, the flowers have three petals and three petal-like sepals. The seeds are contained in large, durable, woody pods. Although there are 450 species of this family found in arid regions worldwide, only one occurs in Wyoming.

Yucca   *Yucca glauca*

Standing like sentinels along roadsides, yuccas have sharply pointed, simple basal leaves. This distinctive plant, also known as *soapweed* and *Spanish bayonet,* has nodding, white or light-green flowers with six similar parts: three petals and three petal-like sepals. Blooming in June and July, the plant grows 36 to 48 inches tall. Native Americans used all parts of this plant: roots for soap, leaves for fiber, and spiny leaf tips as needles.

Look for yucca in sandy soils in the plains and steppe zones on the eastern side of the Continental Divide from North Dakota and Montana to Texas and New Mexico.

BARBERRY FAMILY   Berberidaceae

Often used as landscape plants, members of the barberry family are woody shrubs with spine-tipped, simple or compound leaves, and cup-shaped flowers with six sepals and six petals. The two hundred species in this family occur worldwide in the Northern Hemisphere.

Oregon Grape   *Mahonia repens*

Oregon grape, also called *holly grape,* is a low, creeping, woody shrub that grows 6 to 12 inches tall. Blooming in May and June, its globelike flowers, with six bright yellow petals, grow in showy, round clusters just above the leaves. The glossy, leathery leaves are pinnately compound with three to seven stiff, sharply pointed leaflets that turn bright red in the fall. Resembling small grapes, the clustered fruits, which ripen in late summer, are tart, blue berries with a whitish bloom on their surface. The berries become edible when cooked, and people make juice and jelly out of ripe berries. Native Americans used the roots, stems, and berries of Oregon grape to produce dyes. This is the only species of *Mahonia* native to Wyoming.

Oregon grape grows on dry, rocky slopes in the foothills and montane zones. It is widespread in western North America.

Yucca
Yucca glauca

**Oregon Grape
fruit**
Mahonia repens

**Oregon Grape
flowers**

BELLFLOWER FAMILY   Campanulaceae

The bellflower family includes annual and perennial herbs with simple leaves and bell-shaped flowers with five united petals. It is a large family of about two thousand species that occurs worldwide. There are twelve species in Wyoming.

Harebells   *Campanula*

According to folklore, harebells are known as the flower of witches who used their juices to transform themselves into hares. They have narrow, alternate leaves and grow up to 12 inches tall. The purplish blue to light-blue flowers have five petals united at the base and flared at the tips into an open bell. The genus name is derived from the Latin word *compana,* which means "little bell." There are five species of harebell in Wyoming.

Harebells can be found in sunny meadows and woods in the foothills, montane, subalpine, and alpine zones. They bloom in late June at low elevations to early September in alpine elevations.

Parry's harebell *(Campanula parryi)* has reddish violet flowers held upright on slender stems; the flowers occur singly. Named for Charles Parry, a botanist of the 1849 United States and Mexico Boundary Survey, it grows along moist lake and pond shores and in grassy meadows in the montane zone. This wildflower is found only in the Medicine Bow Range in Wyoming and south into the mountains of Colorado and New Mexico.

Common harebell *(Campanula rotundifolia)*, also known as *bluebell of Scotland,* has small, inconspicuous, round basal leaves and narrow stem leaves. The nodding flowers occur in small, branched clusters on the ends of slender stems. Clumps of this thick and pretty ground cover foster a legend that it provides shelter to fairies. It is a very common wildflower and grows in semi-dry sites in all vegetation zones of Wyoming. It is widespread in western North America.

Alpine harebell *(Campanula uniflora)* is a tiny plant, 4 inches tall, with a single, upward-facing flower nestled in a clump of basal leaves. The blue petals often have a bit of white at the base. Alpine harebell grows only in the alpine zone and occurs from Alaska to Colorado.

Parry's Harebell   *Campanula parryi*

Alpine Harebell   *Campanula uniflora*

Common Harebell   *Campanula rotundifolia*

BORAGE FAMILY   Boraginaceae

The borage family is composed of annual and perennial herbs with over twenty genera in Wyoming and two thousand species worldwide. The leaves are simple and alternate and may be hairless, sparsely hairy, or covered with dense, stiff hair. Flowers have five petals with flaring tips that are united as a tube at their base. The flowers grow in coiled clusters that uncoil and straighten as the flowers open.

Miner's Candle   *Cryptantha*

Plants of this genus have simple, alternate and basal leaves that, in addition to their stems, are densely covered with pointed hair. The foliage is often sticky to the touch and may have sand and dirt embedded in its hairy surface. Flowers have five petals united at the base into a tube; the outer lobes spread flat. The petals are slightly raised around the flower center, forming a distinct eye. Livestock do not graze these plants because of the sharp hair on the foliage.

There are twenty-two species in Wyoming that typically bloom in May and June. Miner's candles are found in dry, sandy, rocky, or gravelly soils in all vegetation zones and are widespread in the western United States.

Tufted cat's-eye (*Cryptantha caespitosa*) grows as a mounded, cushiony mat about 3 inches tall and has whitish flowers that have an orange eye. The leaves are narrow and spoon shaped, and both leaves and stems are covered with soft, woolly, gray hair. It grows in sandy soils in the steppe only in central and southwestern Wyoming into Colorado and Utah.

The whitish, yellow-eyed flowers of **northern miner's candle (*Cryptantha celosioides)*** are clustered along an erect stem that may grow 20 inches tall. The leaves are up to 3 inches long and are spoon shaped. Both stems and leaves are covered with bristly hair. Northern miner's candle is widespread from southern British Columbia and Alberta to Oregon, Colorado, and Nebraska.

Golden miner's candle (*Cryptantha flava*), the only yellow miner's candle in Wyoming, has bright yellow flowers in round to erect clusters on the tips of hairy stems. Leaves grow up to $3^{1}/_{2}$ inches long. They are narrow, elliptical, and densely hairy. Found in sandy soils, this wildflower occurs in the plains and steppe in southern Wyoming and eastern Utah south through Colorado to New Mexico and Arizona.

Northern Miner's Candle
Cryptantha celosioides

Golden Miner's Candle
Cryptantha flava

Tufted Cat's-Eye   *Cryptantha caespitosa*

Alpine Forget-Me-Not   *Eritrichum nanum*

The bright blue flowers of alpine forget-me-not provide a vibrant cushion of color in the alpine zone. This wildflower grows as a compact mat only $1^{1}/_{2}$ inches tall. It has tiny, simple, alternate leaves crowded on short, branched stems. The stems and leaves are covered with short, stiff hair. The flowers have five petals united into a tube with flaring lobes and a yellow and white eye. Common in all high mountains, this is the official flower of Grand Teton National Park. There are two *Eritrichum* species in Wyoming.

Expect to find this unforgettable wildflower on rocky slopes mostly in the alpine zone blooming in June and July. It occurs in Alaska, the Yukon, and the United States Rocky Mountains from Montana to New Mexico.

Stoneseed   *Lithospermum*

Blooming in early spring, these leafy perennials grow 8 to 24 inches tall. They have alternate, narrow, hairy leaves and cream-colored or yellow flowers. The flowers have five petals united into a tube with flaring petal tips. Another common name is *puccoon,* derived from an Algonquin word for blood. The Native Americans used the plants of this genus for red and purple dyes, which they obtained by boiling the plant's roots.

Stoneseeds are found in dry, disturbed soils often along roads. We have described two of the four *Lithospermum* species that are native to Wyoming.

The bright yellow flowers of **plains stoneseed (Lithospermum incisum)** have wavy or slightly fringed petals that unite in a 1-inch-long tube. Widespread and common, it occurs in sandy, gravelly soils in the plains, steppe, and foothills from southern British Columbia, Alberta, and Saskatchewan to Utah and New Mexico.

Western stoneseed (Lithospermum ruderale) has small, pale yellow flowers that are partially hidden among the long, narrow leaves. Look for western stoneseed in open, rocky sites in the steppe, foothills, and montane zones. It occurs from southern British Columbia and Alberta to California, Utah, and western Colorado.

Plains Stoneseed
Lithospermum incisum

Western Stoneseed
Lithospermum ruderale

Alpine Forget-Me-Not   *Eritrichum nanum*

Bluebells *Mertensia*

Bluebells have clusters of truly eye-catching blue flowers at the ends of stems. The leaves are bluish green, simple, and alternate with entire margins. The blue to pinkish blue flowers have five petals united into a narrow, bell-shaped tube with slightly flaring lobes. Pink at bud stage and blue in full bloom, both colors are often evident in the flower clusters. Hikers sometimes eat the leaves of bluebells, which are said to taste like raw peas or oysters. There are nine species in Wyoming.

Bluebells grow on dry, rocky slopes or on moist streambanks in all vegetation zones. They bloom in May in the plains and steppe and as late as August in the subalpine to alpine zones.

Alpine bluebells *(Mertensia alpina)*, generally less than 12 inches tall, has multiple stems with lance-shaped leaves. Royal blue flowers are grouped in upward-facing, erect clusters. It is found only in the alpine zone and occurs from southwestern Montana to New Mexico.

Streamside bluebells *(Mertensia ciliata)* has spreading stems that grow 12 to 48 inches tall with hanging flower clusters. Basal leaves grow up to 6 inches long and are oval, while leaves along the upper stem are elliptical. Seen in bloom from June through August, it is common and widespread west of the Continental Divide. It grows in wet areas along streams in the montane, subalpine, and alpine zones.

Mountain bluebells *(Mertensia viridis)*, usually less than 16 inches tall, has mostly elliptical basal leaves up to 6 inches long and nodding clusters of flowers. Look for this wildflower blooming in May and June. It grows in dry, rocky soils in the upper montane, subalpine, and alpine zones of Montana, Wyoming, Utah, Idaho, and Colorado.

Streamside Bluebells   *Mertensia ciliata*   **Mountain Bluebells**   *Mertensia viridis*

Alpine Bluebells   *Mertensia alpina*

Mountain Forget-Me-Not   *Myosotis alpestris*

This charming wildflower has hairy stems, 4 to 12 inches tall, and alternate, lance-shaped leaves. The sky blue flowers have five petals united as a tube with the outer lobes of the petals spreading flat around a central, yellow eye. Showy and unforgettable, it is the state flower of Alaska. There are two native and four introduced *Myosotis* species in Wyoming.

Mountain forget-me-not blooms in June and July and grows in moist meadows in the subalpine and alpine zones from Alaska to Colorado.

BUCKBEAN FAMILY   Menyanthaceae

This small family of aquatic plants has only thirty species that occur throughout the Northern Hemisphere. The single species of the genus *Menyanthes* occurs in Wyoming. Species of the buckbean family have alternate leaves that are simple or compound. Flowers are regular and have five petals and five sepals. Although the common name indicates a beanlike plant, buckbeans have hard, capsulelike fruits and bitter, inedible leaves.

Buckbean   *Menyanthes trifoliata*

Buckbean, often overlooked unless in bloom, is an aquatic plant that grows in shallow water in large, leafy patches. Its spreading stems have alternate, compound leaves with three oval leaflets, and grow 4 to 12 inches tall. The plant is topped with rounded clusters of showy, white flowers that have five narrow petals fringed with long, branched hair. The petals are sometimes tinged with purple, and purple anthers extend from the center of the flowers.

Buckbean blooms in July and grows in moist, boggy soils and shallow ponds in the montane zone. It grows from Alaska to Colorado, Utah, and Nevada.

BUCKTHORN FAMILY   Rhamnaceae

The buckthorn family contains shrubs and small trees. Species of this family have small flowers with five petals and five sepals. The flowers are grouped in round clusters. Members of this family have alternate leaves that are simple and are not lobed, and some species have thorns. Occurring worldwide, this family is most commonly found in the tropics and subtropics and has fifty-five genera. There are two genera and seven species in Wyoming.

Snowbrush   *Ceanothus velutinus*

Also called *buckbrush,* this thornless evergreen shrub has woody stems that grow 24 to 60 inches tall. Sometimes found in large patches on hillsides, snowbrush has alternate leaves that are broad, oval, and leathery with a shiny upper surface.

Mountain Forget-Me-Not
Myosotis alpestris

Buckbean
Menyanthes trifoliata

Snowbrush *Ceanothus velutinus*

Tiny, fragrant white flowers with five white sepals and five separate, white petals are grouped in showy, dense clusters on branch tips. The presence of these shrubs may indicate that a fire passed through the region at one time since their seeds are fire resistant and remain in the soil for years until heat stimulates them to germinate. Three other *Ceanothus* species also grow in Wyoming.

Snowbrush blooms in June and July and occurs on moist to semimoist hillsides in the foothills and montane zones from southern British Columbia and Alberta to California, Idaho, and Colorado.

BUCKWHEAT FAMILY   Polygonaceae

Most of the plants in the buckwheat family are mat-forming herbs, but there are a few shrubs. Flowers have four, five, or six papery, petal-like sepals and no petals and are grouped in round or umbrella-like clusters on nearly naked stems. Leaves are simple, alternate, and basal. About one thousand species occur worldwide, including the economically important buckwheat (*Fagopyrum sagittatum*) and rhubarb (*Rheum rhaborticum*).

Buckwheat   *Eriogonum*

Growing up to 12 inches tall, the erect stems of buckwheats rise from a broad mat of basal leaves. The foliage is covered with hair, which imparts a gray or white cast to their surface. Their tough leaves are round or spoon shaped with entire margins. Small white, rose, or yellow flowers, with six papery petal-like sepals, grow in flat-topped or rounded clusters at the tips of the stems. The flowers provide nectar for wild bees and the resulting seeds are a food source for smaller rodents and birds. There are twenty *Eriogonum* species in Wyoming, many of which are difficult even for expert botanists to separate and identify.

Buckwheats grow in dry, rocky, open soils in all vegetation zones.

Cushion buckwheat (*Eriogonum ovalifolium*) has oval, grayish green leaves in a cushionlike mat and produces yellow or cream-colored flowers in round, globe-shaped clusters. It flowers in late May to early July. Cushion buckwheat occurs in dry, open sites in all vegetation zones and is widespread in the western United States from southern British Columbia and Alberta to New Mexico.

Wild buckwheat (*Eriogonum umbellatum* var. *majus*) has creeping stems that form extensive mats. Its rounded, leathery leaves are hairy only on the underside. The flowers grow in large, showy, flat-topped, umbrella-like clusters. Though cream colored at first, the flowers turn rose colored as they mature. Flowering in June and July this wildflower grows in all vegetation zones, but most commonly with Wyoming big sagebrush *(Artemisia tridentata)* in the steppe and foothills. In North America, it occurs from British Columbia and Alberta into Colorado.

Sulfur wild buckwheat (*Eriogonum umbellatum* var. *aureum*), a yellow-flowered variety of wild buckwheat, is found in southwestern Wyoming and in the Medicine Bow Range. It also occurs from Montana to Colorado and west to California.

Cushion Buckwheat
Eriogonum ovalifolium

Wild Buckwheat
Eriogonum umbellatum
var. *majus*

Sulfur Wild Buckwheat *Eriogonum umbellatum* var. *aureum*

Alpine Sorrel *Oxyria digyna*

A common wildflower of middle to high elevations, alpine sorrel has fleshy, round or heart-shaped leaves. The foliage is green with dull red to reddish brown overtones. The papery flowers occur in clusters along upright, reddish stems that are 2 to 12 inches tall and have six, greenish red petal-like sepals. Leaves, rich in vitamin C, make a tasty trail snack despite their sour taste.

Growing in moist, rocky areas, often in shallow, running water, alpine sorrel flowers in June and July in the montane, subalpine, and alpine zones. This unique plant, the only species in this genus, is widespread in western North America.

Knotweed *Polygonum*

Adapted to living in water or in very moist soils, plants in this genus have tiny, round flowers in cylindrical flower clusters. The small flowers usually have five white, green, or pink papery, petal-like sepals. There are twenty species in Wyoming occurring in all life zones.

Water ladysthumb *(Polygonum amphibium)*, a strictly aquatic plant, has green to reddish green, simple, elliptical leaves that grow along submerged stems and float on the water's surface. Rosy pink flowers are grouped in rounded clusters held upright above the water. It blooms in July and August and grows in shallow, still water in the plains, steppe, and foothills. It is widespread in western North America.

American bistort *(Polygonum bistortoides)* has white, cylindrical, flower clusters on slender stems 8 to 28 inches tall. The leaves are simple, elliptical to lance shaped, with no teeth. Although mostly basal, there are a few small stem leaves. It blooms from June to early August. Native Americans and early settlers used the starchy root as a food source. Very common at middle to high elevations, it grows in moist areas in the montane, subalpine, and alpine zones from southern British Columbia and Alberta to New Mexico.

Alpine Sorrel *Oxyria digyna*

American Bistort
Polygonum bistortoides

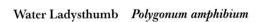

Water Ladysthumb *Polygonum amphibium*

Sorrel *Rumex*

These plants have thick, leathery, simple leaves and pinkish to reddish brown flowers with six papery, petal-like sepals. Flowers grow in erect clusters. There are thirteen species in Wyoming, some of which are large, coarse plants.

They grow in moist to dry habitats, often in disturbed sites, in all vegetation zones.

Mountain sorrel *(Rumex paucifolius)* has basal leaves that often have broken margins, giving this plant a tattered appearance. The small reddish flowers are clustered along upright stems. It blooms from May to July and grows in moist meadows in the montane, subalpine, and alpine zones from southern British Columbia and Alberta to Colorado and west to California.

Sand dock *(Rumex venosus)* grows from creeping underground stems and has alternate, tough, oval leaves. It has flowers made up of three small outer sepals and three large, dark pink, inner petal-like sepals that surround the seed. Sand dock blooms from May to July. Restricted to sandy soils and sand dunes, it lives in the plains and steppe and occurs from southern British Columbia, Alberta, and Saskatchewan to New Mexico and California.

BUR-REED FAMILY   Sparganiaceae

This family of aquatic plants has only one genus with less than twenty species. The plants are distinctive with narrow leaves and unusual, bur-like flower clusters that bear separate male and female flower parts with no petals.

Narrowleaf Bur-Reed *Sparganium angustifolium*

Narrowleaf bur-reed is a perennial aquatic plant that has submerged stems that grow up to 6 feet long and have narrow, grasslike leaves that float horizontally on the water's surface. The small green flowers, appearing in August, occur in round, bur-like clusters on the ends of upright, branched stems. Ducks eat the seeds, and muskrats feed on the entire plant. Four *Sparganium* species occur in Wyoming.

Narrowleaf bur-reed grows in ponds and slow-moving water in the foothills and montane zones. It is widespread in western North America.

Mountain Sorrel
Rumex paucifolius

Narrowleaf Bur-Reed
Sparganium angustifolium

Sand Dock   *Rumex venosus*

BUTTERCUP FAMILY   Ranunculaceae

The buttercup family contains annuals, perennials, and vines. Flowers usually have five separate sepals or petal-like sepals. Petals are absent or vary in number from five to many. There are usually more than ten stamens and three to many pistils. Some flowers are regular in shape and some irregular with sepals modified into a hood or spurs. Some species are poisonous, some ornamental, and some medicinal. Nearly two thousand species occur throughout the cool climate of the Northern Hemisphere.

Monkshood   *Aconitum columbianum*

This picturesque wildflower blooms in moist, mountainous terrain in late July and August. Monkshood has dark blue to nearly white flowers and grows 3 to 7 feet tall. The leaves, growing both at the base and along the stem, are palmately lobed or divided into pointed segments. Flowers occur in erect, open clusters and are irregular in shape with five colored, petal-like sepals and two to five inconspicuous petals. The upper sepal is modified into a hood and covers two winglike side sepals. The two lower sepals are smaller than the others. All parts of this plant contain alkaloids that are poisonous to livestock and humans when eaten. This is the only *Aconitum* species in Wyoming.

Monkshood is common in moist meadows, and along wet streambanks in the foothills, montane, and subalpine zones from southern British Columbia and Montana through the Rocky Mountains to New Mexico.

Western Baneberry   *Actaea rubra*

Western baneberry is distinguished by its glossy, red or white berries that show brightly in the woods in July and August. This spreading leafy plant has palmately compound leaves with three, toothed, sharply pointed, divided leaflets. It grows 12 to 24 inches tall. The white flowers bloom in May and June, have five to ten thin petals that fall off early, and up to fifty stamens. The flowers are grouped in feathery-looking rounded clusters held upright above the leaves. All parts of this plant are known to be poisonous.

Western baneberry is the only *Actaea* species in Wyoming. It grows in moist soils in woods and shady thickets along rivers in the foothills and montane zones. It is widespread in western North America.

Monkshood *Aconitum columbianum*

Western Baneberry fruit *Actaea rubra*

Western Baneberry flower

Windflower *Anemone*

These charming wildflowers bloom early in the spring at lower elevations or just after the snow melts in high alpine zones. The erect plants have opposite, whorled, or basal leaves palmately divided and lobed. The cup-shaped flowers grow on erect stems and lack petals but have colored petal-like sepals. Nine *Anemone* species occur in Wyoming.

Pasqueflower *(Anemone patens)*, also known as *windflower,* has large, deeply cup-shaped, lavender to blue flowers that are up to $1^{1}/_{2}$ inches deep. Flowers are comprised of five to seven petal-like sepals and are hairy on the outside with many yellow stamens in the center. They occur singly on upright stems that grow 4 to 16 inches tall in clumps of silky, hairy leaves. Seen blooming from April to June, pasqueflower is common in the prairie states and is the state flower of South Dakota. It occurs in sandy, well-drained soils in the plains, steppe, foothills, and montane zones east of the Continental Divide from Alaska to Texas.

Teton anemone *(Anemone tetonensis)*, sometimes called *cut-leaved anemone,* has distinctive, solitary flowers with five sepals and many yellow stamens in the center. The long stems, up to 20 inches tall, bear flowers that range from white to rose red. It has basal leaves and whorled leaves below the solitary flower. They are compound with three leaflets that are finely divided again into three parts. Found in the high mountains of northern and western Wyoming, this anemone blooms in July. It occurs from Alaska to New Mexico.

Pasqueflower   *Anemone patens*

Teton Anemone   *Anemone tetonensis*

Columbine   *Aquilegia*

Among our summer favorites, columbines sport large, showy flowers and bluish green foliage. The leaves are mostly basal with a few smaller, alternate leaves along the stem. The large leaves are composed of three leaflets that are further divided into three leaflets for a total of nine leaflets per leaf. Its flowers, on stems 8 to 24 inches tall, are 1 to 2 inches across. They have five colorful, petal-like sepals that extend backward into a spur with a rounded knob on the end. In the center the smaller petals are separate, elliptical, and narrowly spreading. Stamens extend beyond the petals. Nectar produced in the knobbed spurs provides food for hummingbirds. When not in bloom columbine may be confused with meadowrue (*Thalictrum* species). Unlike the nine segments of columbine, the leaves of meadowrue are divided into twenty-seven leaflets.

Six species of columbine occur in Wyoming in moist, sunny locations in the foothills, montane, subalpine, and alpine zones.

Colorado columbine *(Aquilegia coerulea),* the state flower of Colorado, has flowers with spurred sepals in white to blue, and white or light-blue petals. You can find Colorado columbine in the foothills, montane, subalpine, and alpine zones. It blooms from May to early August and occurs from Idaho and Wyoming to New Mexico.

The less common **red columbine *(Aquilegia formosa)*** has red sepals and yellow petals. It blooms in June and July and grows in the mid-montane zone in Yellowstone National Park and occurs from southern British Columbia and Alberta to Idaho, Utah, and Colorado.

Colorado Columbine *Aquilegia coerulea*   **Red Columbine** *Aquilegia formosa*

Marsh Marigold   *Caltha leptosepala*

Often found near melting snow, this wildflower has basal leaves with slightly irregular margins. Plants grow 6 inches tall and have solitary flowers on naked stalks. Flowers have five to fifteen cream-colored, narrow, petal-like sepals and many yellow stamens. The showy flowers that bloom in May to July are $1\frac{1}{2}$ inches or more broad. This is the only *Caltha* species in Wyoming.

Marsh marigold grows in wet, boggy soils and moist meadows in the subalpine and alpine zones and occurs in the Rocky Mountains from southern British Columbia and Alberta to Colorado.

Virgin's Bower   *Clematis*

The usually vinelike, occasionally bushy, plants of the *Clematis* genus have opposite leaves that are pinnately compound with oval, sharp-tipped leaflets. The flowers have four petal-like sepals and numerous stamens. They bloom in May and June with clusters of plumelike, feathery seeds seen late in the season. Ornamental varieties, native to China, are familiar to gardeners as climbing vines with large, colorful flowers. We have described three of the four species found in Wyoming.

Found in somewhat moist soils along rivers in the plains, steppe, foothills, and montane zones, they occur from southern British Columbia and Alberta to Colorado and New Mexico.

Sugar bowl *(Clematis hirsutissima)*, a bushy annual with short stems, grows 12 to 24 inches tall. It has divided, gray, hairy leaves. The nodding purple flowers are vase shaped and are comprised of reflexed, petal-like sepals. Look for sugar bowl in meadows of the foothills and montane zones.

The viney **western virgin's bower *(Clematis ligusticifolia)*** climbs in dense tangles over shrubs, trees, and fences. Its small, $\frac{1}{2}$- to $\frac{3}{4}$-inch-broad white flowers are grouped in rounded clusters. It grows along rivers and roadsides in the plains, steppe, and foothills east of the Continental Divide.

Blue virgin's bower *(Clematis occidentalis)*, a vine that grows up to 15 feet long, has purplish blue to pale purple, nodding, solitary flowers with spreading sepals that are $1\frac{1}{2}$ to $2\frac{1}{2}$ inches long. Found in moist, shady woods in the foothills and montane zones, often along streams, it occurs from southern British Columbia and Alberta to Colorado.

Marsh Marigold *Caltha leptosepala*   **Sugar Bowl** *Clematis hirsutissima*

Western Virgin's Bower
Clematis ligusticifolia

Blue Virgin's Bower
Clematis occidentalis

Larkspur   *Delphinium*

Always eye-catching, larkspurs grow 12 to 60 inches tall and have alternate leaves palmately divided into three, notched lobes. Bright blue to purple flowers are irregular with five purple to dark blue sepals and four small, inconspicuous petals. The upper sepal has a projecting spur. Flowers are grouped in open, erect clusters on tall stems. Larkspurs contain alkaloids, compounds that can poison livestock and cause death if eaten in large amounts.

Nine species of larkspur grow in Wyoming and can be found in dry to moist, sunny sites in all vegetation zones blooming from May through July.

Low larkspur (Delphinium bicolor), seen blooming in early spring, has five spreading, blue sepals and four small petals: two yellowish white with prominent blue lines, and two blue. Flowers grow in sparse, erect, open clusters of four to five blooms. The stems, up to 15 inches tall, are sticky because of glandular hair. Its leaves, round in outline, are palmately divided into three to four narrow segments. It is found in dry, sunny soils in all vegetation zones in central and northern Wyoming, the Black Hills, and north into Montana.

The entirely purplish blue flowers of **Nuttall's larkspur (Delphinium nuttallianum)** have five flaring sepals with four small petals that are notched at their tips. Flowering stems rise from a cluster of basal leaves. The leaves are palmately divided into narrow segments. Growing in dry soils in the steppe, foothills, and montane zones, it occurs from southern British Columbia and Alberta to Colorado.

Tall mountain larkspur (Delphinium occidentale) grows up to 60 inches tall in wet mountain meadows or rocky sites of the montane and subalpine zones. It has sticky, hairy, hollow stems and dark purple flowers up to 1 inch across. Sepals point forward and are not flared out. Leaves are alternate and palmately divided with wide, pointed segments. Tall mountain larkspur occurs from Montana to Colorado.

Top left:
Tall Mountain Larkspur
Delphinium occidentale

Top right:
Low Larkspur
Delphinium bicolor

Bottom right:
Nuttall's Larkspur
Delphinium nuttallianum

Buttercup   *Ranunculus*

The flowers of most buttercups are saucer shaped and have five small sepals, five or more shiny yellow or white petals, and more than ten stamens. The bright green, basal or alternate leaves are simple or compound. Buttercups begin blooming in March in the plains and steppe and continue into July and early August in the alpine zone. Over thirty species of buttercup grow in Wyoming, with the following common ones representing aquatic, moist meadow, and dry steppe habitats.

Look for buttercups in dry and wet soils in all vegetation zones.

Water-plantain buttercup *(Ranunculus alismifolius)*, found in montane, subalpine, and alpine zones in very wet soils, has simple, elliptical leaves up to 6 inches long. Flowers are deeply saucer-shaped with five or more bright yellow petals. It occurs from southern British Columbia and Alberta to California and Colorado.

Water buttercup *(Ranunculus aquatilis)* grows in shallow, slow-moving water and forms large mats of submerged leaves that are divided into narrow, hairlike segments. Stiff stalks hold the pretty white flowers above the water's surface. It occurs in all vegetation zones and is widespread in western North America.

As its common name suggests, **sagebrush buttercup *(Ranunculus glaberrimus)*** is common in the steppe. Often found near melting snowbanks, it is one of the first wildflowers to bloom in early spring. The shiny, waxy, yellow petals often drop before the flower is mature, leaving a rounded center of pistils, stamens, and purplish green sepals. It is the only buttercup in Wyoming that has the unusual feature of having both entire and divided leaves on the same plant. Found in all vegetation zones, it is widespread in western North America.

Floating buttercup *(Ranunculus hyperboreus)* has small, yellow flowers up to $1/2$ inch across and shiny leaves that are palmately compound with three lobed leaflets. Less commonly seen than other buttercups, it floats on shallow ponds and streams in high elevation montane, subalpine, and alpine zones and occurs from Alaska to Colorado and Idaho.

Water-Plantain Buttercup
Ranunculus alismifolius

Water Buttercup
Ranunculus aquatilis

Sagebrush Buttercup
Ranunculus glaberrimus

Floating Buttercup
Ranunculus hyperboreus

Western Meadowrue *Thalictrum occidentale*

A common understory plant along shady riverbanks and aspen stands, western meadowrue has branched stems that grow 12 to 40 inches tall. Its alternate compound leaves are divided into twenty-seven rounded leaflets. Seen blooming in June, the small flowers have no petals, only greenish sepals. Male and female flowers occupy separate plants and hang in drooping, branched clusters. The stamens of the male flower and the pistils of the female flower are prominent. The leaves of western meadowrue resemble columbine (*Aquilegia* species) and the plants can be confused when they are not flowering. Columbine leaves grow mostly at the base of the plant and only have nine leaflets per leaf. Meadowrue has leaves all along its stem with twenty-seven leaflets.

The six Wyoming species of meadowrue are difficult to tell apart. They are common in cool, moist woods in the foothills and montane zones. Western meadowrue is found from southern British Columbia and Alberta to California, Idaho, and Wyoming.

Globeflower *Trollius albiflorus*

Globeflower is aptly named for its rounded, cup-shaped blooms. This low-growing plant inhabits wet areas and grows only 4 to 8 inches tall. The bright green, alternate leaves are palmately divided into five to seven toothed lobes. Its creamy white, cup-shaped flowers, up to 2 inches across, have five to nine round sepals and lack petals. They occur singly on leafy stems. Globeflower is often found blooming with marsh marigold *(Caltha leptosepala),* and they might be confused. However, the leaves of marsh marigold are not lobed, and its petal-like sepals are narrow. This is the only *Trollius* species in Wyoming.

Showy globeflower blooms just after snow melts along moist streambanks and in wet meadows in the montane, subalpine, and alpine zones. In the Rocky Mountains, it can be found from southern British Columbia and Alberta to Idaho and Colorado.

Western Meadowrue (male)   Western Meadowrue (female)

Thalictrum occidentale

Globeflower *Trollius albiflorus*

CACTUS FAMILY   Cactaceae

Common in dry habitats, the perennial plants of this family have fleshy stems with sharp spines instead of leaves. Showy, brightly colored flowers are regular with many sepals, petals, and stamens. There are about two thousand species of cactus worldwide, with most occurring in the dry, warm areas of North and South America. Seven species occur in Wyoming.

Plains Prickly Pear Cactus   *Opuntia polyacantha*

This cactus has fleshy, flattened stem segments covered with 1-inch spines. The segments are 1 to 5 inches long and break apart easily. Showy, yellow to pinkish, bowl-shaped flowers are 2 inches or more across when fully open and have many thin, almost translucent, petals. Oval fruits are deep pink to brick red when ripe. Early settlers and Native Americans ate both stems and fruits when food was scarce. Four species of prickly pear cactus occur in Wyoming.

Blooming in June, it covers large areas of overgrazed land in the plains, steppe, and foothills from southern Canada to New Mexico.

Mountain Ball Cactus   *Coryphantha vivipara*

Mountain ball, also called *pincushion cactus,* has round, ball-shaped stems with spines clustered on rounded bumps (tubercles). Growing either alone or in clusters, the stems are only 4 inches tall and 2 to 3 inches across with pink flowers at the tips of the tubercles. Two species of ball cactus occur in Wyoming and bloom in May.

Mountain ball cactus inhabits open areas, often on powdery soils. Found in the plains, steppe, and foothills in eastern Wyoming, it occurs from southern Alberta to Colorado.

Plains Prickly Pear Cactus   *Opuntia polyacantha*

Mountain Ball Cactus   *Coryphantha vivipara*

CAPER FAMILY   Capparaceae

Members of the caper family are annuals or shrubby perennials with showy, brightly colored flowers with four sepals, four petals, and six stamens that extend well beyond the petals. Although there are eight hundred species worldwide, only two genera and four species occur in Wyoming.

Beeplant   *Cleome*

Flowering in August and September, this tall, robust annual with fibrous, well-branched stems grows up to 48 inches tall. It has palmately compound, alternate leaves with three to five leaflets. The flowers are arranged in rounded clusters, each with four petals and six stamens. The stamens are twice as long as the petals and extend well beyond them. The flowers open in succession from the bottom of the flower cluster to the top. The capsulelike fruits that ripen below the cluster resemble pods of the pea family. Beeplant produces plenty of nectar and is a favorite forage plant of bees. We have described two of the three species that occur in Wyoming.

Beeplants grow in dry, gravelly soils along roadsides and other disturbed sites in the plains and steppe.

Yellow beeplant *(Cleome lutea)* has yellow flowers and leaves with five leaflets and occurs from Washington and Montana to New Mexico.

Rocky Mountain beeplant *(Cleome serrulata)* has rosy pink flowers and leaves with three leaflets and occurs from southern British Columbia, Alberta, and Saskatchewan to New Mexico and Arizona.

Yellow Beeplant
Cleome lutea

Rocky Mountain Beeplant
Cleome serrulata

CARROT FAMILY   Apiaceae

The carrot family, also known as the *parsley family,* has nearly three thousand species distributed worldwide; they occur most commonly in the Northern Hemisphere. Characterized by small flowers with five petals that grow in flat-topped, umbrella-like clusters, this family of common plants includes medicinal, edible, and poisonous species. Do not ingest any carrot family plants without positive identification since some members are poisonous, even deadly, and are easily confused with plants that are not poisonous. Consult a technical flora or ask a professional botanist for help with identifications before consuming any plants of this family.

Pinnate-Leaved Angelica   *Angelica pinnata*

This robust plant grows up to 36 inches tall and has alternate, pinnately compound leaves. Leaflets, 1 to 3 inches long, are lance shaped with fine teeth on their margins. The small, green to pink flowers are arranged in flat-topped, umbrella-like clusters. Angelica is often brewed as an herbal tea or used as a parsleylike garnish. It blooms in midsummer from late June to early August. Five *Angelica* species occur in Wyoming.

Pinnate-leaved angelica grows in wet soils, often along rivers, in the montane and subalpine zones in the northwestern Wyoming, southwestern Montana, and eastern Idaho. It occurs west of the Continental Divide from Montana to New Mexico.

Plains Spring Parsley   *Cymopterus acaulis*

Plains spring parsley, one of the first wildflowers to bloom in spring, has parsleylike, compound basal leaves and single stems that grow up to 4 inches tall. The grayish white flowers are arranged in dense, flat-topped clusters that are $1^1/_2$ inches across. Of the thirteen species of spring parsley in Wyoming this parsley is one of the most common. Spring parsley is a difficult group to identify because it closely resembles desert parsley (*Lomatium* species), another group that is difficult to identify. These two genera are most easily separated by microscopic characteristics.

Plains spring parsley grows in sandy and gravelly soil in the plains, steppe, and foothills from southern Alberta and Saskatchewan to Texas.

Cow Parsnip   *Heracleum sphondylium*

Cow parsnip is a large, robust plant that grows up to 5 feet tall and has large, showy, maplelike leaves. The leaves are palmately compound, 4 to 12 inches across, and possess three divided, or lobed, leaflets. Several clusters of small white flowers are grouped together in a large, flat-topped cluster that is 4 to 12 inches across. The reddish stem is coarse and hairy, and may cause skin

Plains Spring Parsley   *Cymopterus acaulis*

Pinnate-Leaved Angelica
Angelica pinnata

Cow Parsnip
Heracleum sphondylium

irritation when handled. Native Americans ate this nonpoisonous member of the carrot family.

Cow parsnip, the only *Heracleum* species in Wyoming, blooms in July and August and grows in moist soils, often along streams in the foothills, montane, subalpine, and alpine zones. It is widespread in western North America.

Lovage *Ligusticum*

Typical of the carrot family, lovage flowers are small with white petals and are grouped in flat-topped, umbrella-like clusters. The plants have a base covered in dry leaf stalks, nearly naked stems, and fernlike, pinnately compound leaves. Basal leaves grow up to 8 inches long, and smaller leaves with fewer leaflets grow along the stem. It grows 24 to 48 inches tall. Lovage has a distinct celery-like odor. It is popular in herbal medicine, and because of this wild populations are being depleted through overcollection.

Four species occur in Wyoming and bloom in June and July. Lovage grows in partial shade in moist soils of the montane and subalpine zones.

The leaves of **fernleaf lovage (*Ligusticum filicinum*)** are finely divided into narrow, threadlike segments less than ⅛ inch across. It grows along streambanks in the montane and subalpine zones in the Absaroka, Teton, and Beartooth Ranges and occurs in Montana, Idaho, and Wyoming.

The leaves of **Porter's lovage (*Ligusticum porteri*)** are divided into broader segments that are up to ¼ inch wide. Also called *osha,* it grows in partly moist soils of the montane zone in the Medicine Bow Range. It occurs from Montana to Arizona and New Mexico.

Desert Parsley *Lomatium*

These wildflowers have pinnately compound leaves and small, yellow or white flowers in flat-topped, umbrella-like clusters. There are thirteen species in Wyoming that occur in all vegetation zones and flower from May to July.

Fernleaf desert parsley (*Lomatium dissectum*), which grows 18 to 36 inches tall, has finely divided basal leaves, bright yellowish green flowers and reddish, hollow stems. The showy, flat-topped flower clusters spread 3 to 4 inches across. It grows in full sun in dry, rocky soils in the foothills and lower montane zones and occurs from southern British Columbia and Alberta to Colorado.

Nineleaf biscuitroot (*Lomatium triternatum*) is a slender plant with pale yellow flowers in open, sparse, flat-topped clusters on branched stems. It grows 8 to 32 inches tall and has leaves divided into nine slender leaflets. Nineleaf biscuitroot grows on dry, rocky, exposed hillsides in the steppe and foothills from southern British Columbia and Alberta to Colorado.

Fernleaf Lovage
Ligusticum filicinum

Porter's Lovage
Ligusticum porteri

Fernleaf Desert Parsley
Lomatium dissectum

Nineleaf Biscuitroot
Lomatium triternatum

Slender Wild Parsley *Musineon tenuifolium*

This leafy plant grows up to 12 inches tall with spreading basal leaves. The finely divided leaves are pinnately compound with narrow, pinnately lobed leaflets. Blooming in May, the tiny yellow flowers are grouped in compact, flat-topped clusters. Native Americans used the bitter tasting roots as a survival food during long winters. Three species occur in Wyoming.

Slender wild parsley is found in rocky or sandy soil in the plains and steppe zones and occurs in western South Dakota, eastern Wyoming, northwestern Nebraska, and northeastern Colorado.

Common Yampah *Perideridia montana*

The fleshy, carrotlike roots of common yampah were an important food source for Native Americans, trappers, and early settlers. It has slender, solitary stems that grow 16 to 36 inches tall with leaves pinnately divided into long, narrow leaflets. Before the flowers appear, the few stem leaves often dry and fall off. The tiny white flowers are grouped in flat-topped, open clusters. Two *Perideridia* species occur in Wyoming.

Common yampah is found in the plains, steppe, and foothills from British Columbia and Alberta to New Mexico.

CATTAIL FAMILY Typhaceae

Composed of aquatic, perennial plants, the cattail family has nine species and only one genus. They are found worldwide in temperate and tropical zones. Two species occur in Wyoming.

Cattail *Typha*

Cattails are aquatic plants that grow 3 to 6 feet tall and have stiff, flat, strap-shaped leaves. In late spring and early summer tiny flowers without sepals and petals form in fuzzy, greenish brown, erect, cylindrical clusters, or *cattails*. The cattails turn brown as they mature, dry out, and persist through the fall. Native Americans ate the fleshy underground stems.

Cattails can be found in sloughs and marshes in the plains, steppe, and foothills in the western United States.

Narrowleaf cattail *(Typha angustifolia)* has leaves that are about ¹/₂ inch wide and slender cattails that are ³/₄ inch broad and up to 7 inches tall. Where their ranges overlap, it sometimes grows with **broadleaf cattail *(Typha latifolia)*.** The broadleaf cattail has leaves ¹/₂ to ³/₄ inch wide and shorter, fatter cattails that are 1¹/₄ inches broad and up to 4 inches long.

Slender Wild Parsley *Musineon tenuifolium*

Common Yampah
Perideridia montana

Below right: Narrowleaf Cattail
Typha angustifolia
Below left: Broadleaf Cattail
Typha latifolia

CURRANT FAMILY   Grossulariaceae

The currant family, also called the *gooseberry family,* has 350 species in a single genus worldwide. All members are shrubs with smooth stems or stems covered with spines or prickles. The colored, tubular flowers have five united sepals and inconspicuous petals that produce colorful berries. Ten species occur in Wyoming.

Currant and Gooseberry   *Ribes*

Currants have smooth stems, and gooseberries have stems armed with short spines or prickles. They are small, woody shrubs common in moist sites and grow 48 to 60 inches tall. Bright green, maplelike, alternate leaves are palmately divided into rounded lobes. The small tubular flowers, hanging in clusters along the stems, have five united, colored sepals with flaring tips and inconspicuous petals. Depending on the species, the berries may be tasteless and bitter or sour and succulent; the sour and succulent berries are excellent for making jelly.

Currants and gooseberries flower during May and early June and grow along streambanks in all vegetation zones throughout the western United States and Canada.

Golden currant (*Ribes aureum*) is an especially attractive shrub, particularly in fall when its leaves turn bright red. It can grow up to 60 inches tall and is the only native currant with golden yellow flowers. The smooth, dark purple berries are good for juice and jelly. Golden currant grows along streams in the plains, steppe, and foothills.

Wax currant (*Ribes cereum*) has clusters of two to eight pink flowers. Its leaves have round lobes and are often sticky and hairy. The red berries have protruding, sticky hair and are bitter and tasteless. It is found on dry slopes in all vegetation zones.

The young stems of **whitestem gooseberry (*Ribes inerme*)** are covered with sharp spines while the older, white-barked stems have fewer spines. Flowers of this plant are white with protruding stamens and develop into dark purple berries. Whitestem gooseberry is the alternate host for white pine blister rust *(Cronartium ribicola),* a fungal infection that was introduced from Europe in the early 1900s. At one time foresters tried, unsuccessfully, to eradicate this plant from the western forests in an effort to save western white pine *(Pinus monticola).* Whitestem gooseberry grows in moist areas in the foothills and montane zones.

Mountain gooseberry (*Ribes montigenum*) has spiny stems, sticky leaves, dark pink flowers, and red berries. It occurs in rocky soils in the subalpine and alpine zones.

Golden Currant *Ribes aureum*

Wax Currant *Ribes cereum*
Inset: Wax Currant fruit

Whitestem Gooseberry
Ribes inerme

Mountain Gooseberry
Ribes montigenum

DOGBANE FAMILY   Apocynaceae

The dogbane family is composed of plants with milky juice, simple opposite leaves, and tubular flowers with five united petals. The one-thousand-plus species are mostly tropical and subtropical. Some dogbanes are used commercially in the production of rubber.

Spreading Dogbane   *Apocynum androsaemifolium*

Spreading dogbane, a perennial with 8- to 30-inch stems that die back to the ground each season, grows in large patches. Its opposite leaves are elliptical with pointed tips. Pink, bell-shaped flowers, are composed of five united, re-curved petals, and form clusters on the branch tips. When cut, stems and leaves ooze a milky sap that contains a glycoside, a compound that may make animals and people sick if they ingest it. Two *Apocynum* species occur in Wyoming.

    Spreading dogbane blooms in July and August. It grows in well-drained sites in the plains, steppe, foothills, and montane zones and is widespread in western North America.

DOGWOOD FAMILY   Cornaceae

The dogwood family of one hundred species contains shrubs and trees that occur only in northern temperate climates. The flowers have four sepals, four petals, four stamens and simple, opposite or whorled leaves.

Dogwood   *Cornus*

Red-osier dogwood and bunchberry have flowers grouped in rounded clusters that bloom in June and July. They have opposite or whorled, oval to elliptical leaves with entire margins. Their showy berries are not poisonous but may have a bitter taste. Two species occur in Wyoming.

    They grow in moist areas in the foothills and montane zones.

    Bunchberry *(Cornus canadensis)* grows 4 inches tall and has four whorled leaves per stem and six whorled leaves below the flower cluster. Four white, leaflike bracts, which look like petals, surround clusters of small, green flowers. Bright red berries grow in an erect cluster. It is found in moist, coniferous forests of the foothills and montane zones from Alaska to New Mexico.

    Red-osier dogwood *(Cornus sericea)* is a shrub that grows 3 to 6 feet tall. It has red bark and opposite branches and leaves. The small white flowers are massed in flat-topped clusters at the branch tips. Deer love its leaves and wildlife eat its bluish white berries. It grows along streambanks in the plains, steppe, foothills, and montane zones throughout the western United States.

Spreading Dogbane
Apocynum androsaemifolium

Bunchberry
Cornus canadensis
Inset:
Bunchberry fruit

Red-Osier Dogwood
Cornus sericea

EVENING-PRIMROSE FAMILY   Onagraceae

Most members of the evening-primrose family are perennial or biennial herbs. They occur in the Northern Hemisphere, mostly in North America, with the greatest diversity of species occurring in the western United States. The large flowers, comprised of four sepals, four petals, and eight stamens, open at dusk and are pollinated by moths. There are over forty species in Wyoming.

Fireweed   *Chamerion angustifolium*

This common wildflower has bright magenta flowers in erect clusters. The flowers have four petals and eight stamens and begin blooming from the bottom of the cluster to the top. Alternate, lance-shaped leaves are bright green and smooth. Its narrow, elongate pods release seeds attached to fine, silky hair that allows the seeds to float with the wind. This wildflower blooms from June through August. Two species occur in Wyoming.

Fireweed, formerly called *Epilobium angustifolium,* is one of the first wildflowers to bloom after a forest fire. It grows in the foothills, montane, subalpine, and alpine zones and is widespread in western North America.

Alpine Willowherb   *Epilobium clavatum*

Alpine willowherb is a short bushy plant of wet areas that grows up to 12 inches tall. Its narrow, willowlike, alternate leaves have a reddish cast. The small, light-pink flowers, with four, notched petals and eight stamens, grow along the upper stems. Fourteen *Epilobium* species grow in Wyoming.

Alpine willowherb blooms in July and August and is found along streams in the subalpine and alpine zones; it occurs from northern Alaska to Idaho and Colorado.

Scarlet Butterfly Flower   *Gaura coccinea*

Scarlet butterfly flower is named for its small, slightly irregular blooms that have strap-shaped, reflexed, winglike petals. The stems are 8 to 12 inches tall and have narrow, alternate leaves covered with white hair that gives them a grayish green color. The pink or apricot-colored flowers have four petals and eight stamens that extend out beyond them; the flowers are grouped in narrow clusters. The individual flowers of scarlet butterfly flower bloom for less than a day. They open in the late afternoon, are pollinated by moths at night, and close the next morning. Three species of butterfly flower occur in Wyoming. Colorado butterfly flower *(Gaura neomexicana)* is a sensitive and threatened species that occurs in southeastern Wyoming and northeastern Colorado. It has white flowers that turn pink as they wither and age.

Scarlet butterfly flower blooms in May and June and grows in dry, disturbed soils in the plains, steppe, and foothills. It occurs in the Great Plains south to Mexico and west to Montana and Wyoming.

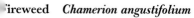

Fireweed *Chamerion angustifolium*

Scarlet Butterfly Flower *Gaura coccinea*

Alpine Willowherb *Epilobium clavatum*

Evening Primrose *Oenothera*

Evening primroses, wildflowers of the night, have large, short-lived, showy flowers with four rounded petals and eight stamens. Evening-primrose flowers open late in the afternoon or evening and close the following morning. They are adapted for insect pollination, and their fragrance and sweet nectar attract hawkmoths and other night-flying insects. Twelve species occur in Wyoming.

Evening primroses bloom in May, June, and July and grow in dry, sandy, or gravelly areas, often along roadsides, in all vegetation zones.

Tufted evening-primrose *(Oenothera cespitosa)* is stemless and has flowers nestled in a basal cluster of lance-shaped leaves. They are entire or have ragged teeth and grow 1 to 10 inches long. The white flowers, 2 to 3 inches broad, turn pink as they wither. This showy wildflower occurs in dry, gravelly, or clay soils, often along roads, in all vegetation zones and is widespread in western North America.

Stemless evening-primrose *(Oenothera flava)* has basal leaves with backward-pointing notches and bright yellow flowers that are 1 inch across. It grows on seasonally moist clay flats near the shoreline of reservoirs and lakes and is found in the plains, steppe, foothills, and montane zones. It occurs from the western Great Plains to Oregon, California, and Arizona.

Nuttall's evening-primrose *(Oenothera nuttallii)* is a branched, compact plant with white flowers, 1 to 2 inches broad, on whitish to reddish stems up to 15 inches tall. Nuttall's evening-primrose has an unpleasant fragrance. It occurs in dry, sandy, gravelly soils in the steppe and foothills, often along roadsides, mostly east of the Continental Divide from southern British Columbia and Alberta to South Dakota, Wyoming, and Colorado.

Hairy evening-primrose *(Oenothera villosa)* has stiff, leafy, hairy stems, up to 30 inches tall, with yellow flowers that grow up to 2 inches broad. It occurs in disturbed, semimoist soils in the plains, steppe, and lower foothills and is widespread in the northern Great Plains west to the Continental Divide.

Tufted Evening-Primrose
Oenothera cespitosa

Stemless Evening-Primrose
Oenothera flava

Nuttall's Evening-Primrose
Oenothera nuttallii

Hairy Evening-Primrose
Oenothera villosa

FIGWORT FAMILY　　　　　　　　　　Scrophulariaceae

The figwort family is conspicuous in the western United States due to its diversity of species, widespread occurrence, and showy flowers. Plants have alternate or opposite, simple to deeply divided leaves. The colorful, irregular flowers have four to five united sepals and four to five petals that are united into a tube with upper and lower lips. Adapted for insect pollination, flower color and shape guide insects to reproductive parts in the center of the flowers. This large family contains three thousand species worldwide.

Wyoming Kittentails　*Besseya wyomingensis*

Wyoming kittentails has tiny, petal-less flowers in dense, cylindrical, fuzzy-looking clusters, hence the common name. The purple stamens that protrude beyond the green bracts give the flower its color. The plant, 4 to 10 inches tall, has hairy stems and oval, toothed leaves. Three species of *Besseya* occur in Wyoming.

Wyoming kittentails blooms from April to May and grows in dry, rocky sites in the plains, steppe, and foothills. In western North America, it occurs from southern British Columbia and Alberta to Nebraska, Colorado, and Utah.

Indian Paintbrush　*Castilleja*

Indian paintbrushes are well known and easily recognized. More than fifteen species of these variously colored wildflowers are common and abundant in Wyoming. Altogether, there are two hundred species of *Castilleja,* and almost all occur in western North America. Indian paintbrushes have small irregular flowers mostly hidden by colored, leafy bracts. The flowers have petals that are united into upper and lower lips. The species are difficult to separate and most are distinguished by habitat, color, size of the petals, and other microscopic characteristics. Flowers vary in color from white and yellow to all shades of red and pink and are grouped in terminal clusters that look like they have been dipped in paint.

Indian paintbrushes are partial parasites, using sagebrush or grasses to supply part of their water and mineral requirements. They grow in dry to moist sites in all vegetation zones.

Narrowleaf Indian paintbrush (Castilleja angustifolia), a very common associate of Wyoming big sagebrush (*Artemisia tridentata*), may be found in a range of colors from yellow to orange to red. Plants grow up to 12 inches tall with narrow leaves that are 2 inches long and may have three spreading lobes. Plants of different colors often grow in the same area. It blooms in May and June and occurs in steppe and foothills throughout the western United States.

Wyoming Kittentails
Besseya wyomingensis

Narrowleaf Indian Paintbrush
Castilleja angustifolia

Yellow Indian paintbrush *(Castilleja flava)* has bright yellow flowers on branched stems. Leaves are narrow with three segments and stems grow up to 15 inches tall. Blooming in June to August, it is found in the steppe in central and western Wyoming and southwestern Montana to Oregon and Nevada.

Wyoming Indian paintbrush *(Castilleja linariifolia),* the official state flower of Wyoming, has leafy, red bracts with protruding, yellow flowers. Stems grow up to 24 inches tall with narrow, divided leaves up to 3 inches long. It blooms in July and August and occurs on dry slopes in the steppe, foothills, and montane zones from Montana to New Mexico.

Top:
Yellow Indian
Paintbrush
Castilleja flava

Bottom:
Wyoming Indian
Paintbrush
Castilleja linariifolia

Scarlet Indian paintbrush *(Castilleja miniata)* is perhaps the most common red paintbrush of the mid-montane and subalpine zones in western North America. It grows 24 inches tall and has narrow, entire leaves that are about 2 inches long. Blooming in July and August, dense clumps of scarlet Indian paintbrush occur in moist meadows and along streams.

The petite **showy Indian paintbrush *(Castilleja pulchella)*** occurs only in the subalpine and alpine zones. It grows about 3 inches tall and has lance-shaped, lobed leaves about 1 inch long. The flowers bloom in June, July, and August and are cream colored or light pink. It grows in moist, mountain meadows and occurs only in western Montana, northwestern Wyoming, eastern Idaho, and in Utah's Uinta Mountains.

Rosy Indian paintbrush *(Castilleja rhexifolia)*, very common in the subalpine and alpine zones, has rosy pink to purplish crimson flowers. Plants grow 24 inches tall and have lance-shaped, entire leaves that are 3 inches long. It blooms in late July and August and is widespread across the western United States.

Sulfur Indian paintbrush *(Castilleja sulphurea)* has smooth, lance-shaped, entire leaves that are 2 inches long, and large, leafy, cream-colored to greenish yellow flower clusters. Plants grow up to 18 inches tall. Sulfur Indian paintbrush blooms in July and grows in open patches in meadows and aspen groves in the subalpine and alpine zones of the Rocky Mountains from southern British Columbia and Alberta to New Mexico.

Scarlet Indian Paintbrush
Castilleja miniata

Showy Indian Paintbrush
Castilleja pulchella

Rosy Indian Paintbrush
Castilleja rhexifolia

Sulfur Indian Paintbrush
Castilleja sulphurea

Monkeyflower *Mimulus*

Monkeyflowers are herbaceous plants that have leafy, branched stems with opposite leaves that are oval to elliptical and have coarse teeth on their margins. The showy, irregular flowers are comprised of five, spotted petals united into a monkeylike face. The flowers are trumpet shaped with a tube and two flaring lips; the upper lip is notched into two lobes, the lower lip into three lobes. Thirteen species grow in Wyoming.

Monkeyflowers grow in wet meadows, swamps, and streamsides in the foothills, montane, subalpine, and alpine zones.

Yellow monkeyflower *(Mimulus guttatus)* has large, yellow flowers, $1^{1}/_{2}$ inches long, with purple dots in their throat. Leaves are oval and 2 inches long. The plant grows up to 18 inches tall and blooms June to August. It is quite common and is widespread in western North America.

Lewis's monkeyflower *(Mimulus lewisii)* has dark pink flowers that are $1^{1}/_{2}$ inches long and have a yellow throat. The plants may reach 30 inches tall and have opposite, oval leaves that grow up to 3 inches long. It was named for Meriwether Lewis of the Lewis and Clark Expedition who first collected it for science in 1805. Found along streams in the subalpine and alpine zones, Lewis's monkeyflower blooms in July and August. It occurs from British Columbia south through the Rocky Mountains to Colorado.

Owlclover *Orthocarpus luteus*

Owlclover is an herbaceous annual with slender, mostly unbranched stems that grow up to 12 inches tall. The narrow, alternate leaves are pressed close to the reddish stems, which are hairy and slightly sticky to the touch. Its flowers are yellow, irregular, and grow in dense, erect clusters. Three species occur in Wyoming.

Owlclover blooms in July and August and grows in sandy prairies and gravelly roadsides in the plains, steppe, foothills, and montane zones throughout the western United States.

Yellow Monkeyflower
Mimulus guttatus

Owlclover
Orthocarpus luteus

Lewis's Monkeyflower   *Mimulus lewisii*

Lousewort *Pedicularis*

Louseworts usually grow at high elevations and have brightly colored, irregular flowers. They have tall, leafy stems, 6 to 27 inches tall, with alternate leaves that are entire, toothed, deeply divided or pinnately lobed. The flowers grow in dense, erect clusters and have petals united into upper and lower lips. The upper lip is usually hoodlike and often curved into a projecting point (beak). The lower lip is rounded or lobed. The common name lousewort comes from an old European belief that cattle grazing on these plants would get lice.

Ten species of lousewort occur in moist soils in the steppe, foothills, montane, subalpine, and alpine zones.

Fernleaf lousewort (*Pedicularis bracteosa*) has finely divided, fernlike leaves that are five inches long and pale yellow flowers tinged pink. The upper lip forms a hood, and the downturned lower lip has rounded lobes. It blooms in June and July. Fernleaf lousewort grows in moist or partially dry soils in the montane, subalpine, and alpine zones west of the Great Plains and is widespread in forests throughout western North America.

Meadow lousewort (*Pedicularis crenulata*) has leaves that are merely scalloped, not divided. Its magenta flowers have a long, hooded upper lip and a broadly round lower lip. It blooms in June and July and can be found growing over large areas in wet meadows. It occurs in the steppe, foothills, and montane zones only in Wyoming, Colorado, Nevada, and eastern California.

A most unusual plant, **elephant head lousewort (*Pedicularis groenlandica*)** has small pink flowers that resemble elephant heads. The upper petal has a beaked projection that resembles an elephant's trunk, and the flared, lower petals resemble the ears. The mostly basal leaves are divided pinnately and grow up to 7 inches long. It blooms in June and July, grows in wet to moist meadows in the montane, subalpine, and alpine zones, and is widespread in western North America.

Parry's lousewort (*Pedicularis parryi*) has mostly basal leaves and pale yellow flowers that have a rounded upper petal with a short beak and a rounded lower lip. Seen flowering in July it grows in moist meadows in the subalpine and alpine zones from southwestern Montana and eastern Utah to Colorado.

Fernleaf Lousewort
Pedicularis bracteosa

Meadow Lousewort
Pedicularis crenulata

Elephant Head Lousewort
Pedicularis groenlandica

Parry's Lousewort
Pedicularis parryi

Beardtongue *Penstemon*

Across the region these striking wildflowers brighten the roadsides. *Penstemon* is one of the largest genera in the western United States with about 250 species. Within Wyoming there are over forty species, from diminutive plants with small flowers to large, robust specimens. We have described seven of the more common species. In general, many of the species are similar in appearance and are difficult to differentiate without using microscopic characteristics. These descriptions are intended to illustrate genus variations and to help readers recognize a wildflower as a beardtongue.

All beardtongues have simple, opposite leaves and irregular flowers with five petals united in a two-lipped tube; each lip is divided into lobes. The flowers are clustered along erect stems. Although most species are various shades of blue, a few species are pink or white. The flowers have a sterile stamen that is bearded, usually with yellow hair, hence the common name.

Beardtongues usually grow in dry, disturbed soils in all vegetation zones in the western United States.

**Narrowleaf beardtongue (*Penstemon angustifolius)* blooms in May on the plains and grows up to 15 inches tall. Its narrow, smooth, and glossy leaves, up to 4 inches long, have no teeth on their margins. Narrowleaf beardtongue has blue flowers with a white throat and blooms in May and June. It grows in sandy soils in the plains in eastern Wyoming, western South Dakota, and eastern Montana to New Mexico and Arizona.

**Fuzzy-tongued beardtongue (*Penstemon eriantherus)* grows up to 12 inches tall. Its sticky, glandular, elliptical leaves are toothed and grow up to 4 inches long. Its flowers are pale lavender with a prominent bearded stamen displayed in the throat. They bloom in June and grow in elongate, dense, erect clusters. Fuzzy-tongued beardtongue grows in sandy, dry soils along roads in the plains, steppe, and foothills from western Nebraska and eastern Wyoming to Oregon.

**Western smooth beardtongue (*Penstemon glaber)* is an eye-catching plant that grows up to 24 inches tall. It has white-throated blue flowers that grow up to 1½ inches long. The large, elliptical leaves, up to 3 inches long, have wavy edges. It blooms in May and June, grows in gravelly soil in the plains, steppe, and foothills, and occurs from North Dakota to Montana and Colorado.

**Low beardtongue (*Penstemon humilis)* is a small, 10-inch plant with narrow leaves up to 2 inches long. It bears whorls of diminutive blue flowers that are ½ inch long. Low beardtongue blooms in May and June. Although common in steppe, it is also found in the foothills, montane, subalpine, and alpine zones from central Wyoming to Washington and Oregon.

Narrowleaf Beardtongue
Penstemon angustifolius

Fuzzy-Tongued Beardtongue
Penstemon eriantherus

Western Smooth Beardtongue
Penstemon glaber

Low Beardtongue
Penstemon humilis

Rydberg's beardtongue *(Penstemon rydbergii)* grows up to 16 inches tall, has bright royal blue flowers in dense whorls, and blooms in June and July. The leaves are simple, elliptical, entire, and grow up to 3 inches long. It grows in moist to partly dry meadows in the foothills, montane, subalpine, and alpine zones and occurs in southwestern Montana, Wyoming, Utah, Idaho, and Colorado. It is named for Per Axel Rydberg, a botanist who surveyed the Rocky Mountains and Great Plains for the United States Department of Agriculture and the New York Botanic Garden in the late 1800s and early 1900s.

Smooth beardtongue *(Penstemon subglaber)* has smooth, entire, elliptical leaves and grows up to 15 inches tall, though it may be taller in some habitats. The flowers are two-tone with light-blue tubes and brighter blue flaring lips. It blooms in June and July and is found in gravelly soils in the steppe, foothills, and montane zones only in western Wyoming and eastern Utah.

Whipple's beardtongue *(Penstemon whippleanus)* has hairy stems and dark purple (or sometimes cream-colored), hairy flowers that are 1 inch long. It grows up to 12 inches tall. The lance-shaped, entire leaves are 1 to $2^1/_2$ inches long. Whipple's beardtongue blooms in July and August and can be found in spruce-fir forests in high-elevation montane and subalpine zones. It occurs from southwestern Montana through western and southern Wyoming into Colorado and Utah.

Alpine Speedwell   *Veronica wormskjoldii*

Although alpine speedwell is quite common, it is a small plant and is easily overlooked. The stems are slender and short, 2 to 12 inches tall, and have glandular hair. It has opposite, small, egg-shaped leaves with smooth margins. The small, irregular flowers have dark blue petals united into a short tube and grow in clusters along the upper stem. It blooms in mid-July to August. Alpine speedwell is edible and has been used in herbal medicines to treat a variety of ailments. There are six native species and six introduced species of speedwell in Wyoming.

Alpine speedwell grows in moist meadows in the subalpine and alpine zones and is widespread in western North America.

Rydberg's Beardtongue
Penstemon rydbergii

Smooth Beardtongue
Penstemon subglaber

Whipple's Beardtongue
Penstemon whippleanus

Alpine Speedwell
Veronica wormskjoldii

FLAX FAMILY   Linaceae

The flax family is comprised of annual or perennial herbs that have colorful flowers of five petals and simple, slender leaves. It is best known for the cultivated plant *Linum usitatissimum* that people grow for linen fibers and linseed oil. There are 220 species worldwide in temperate climates.

Flax   *Linum*

Flax plants have slender stems that grow 10 to 24 inches tall and have narrow, alternate leaves. The regular, saucer-shaped flowers have five separate, rounded petals and five stamens. Opening in the morning, the petals usually drop by midday.

Species of flax grow in dry soils in all vegetation zones. They bloom June through August. Six species occur in Wyoming.

King's flax (*Linum kingii*) has yellow flowers that are about 1 inch broad and occur in rounded clusters on crowded, spreading stems. Leaves are narrow and about ½ inch long. King's flax favors limestone soils and occurs in the steppe, foothills, montane, and subalpine zones from central Wyoming into Utah and Colorado.

Blue flax (*Linum lewisii*) has sky blue petals with white or yellowish bases. The flowers occur on slender, waving stems. Leaves are linear and about 1 inch long. Named in honor of Meriwether Lewis, this plant was first collected for science on the Lewis and Clark expedition in 1805. It is found throughout western North America and is common in all vegetation zones.

King's Flax   *Linum kingii*

Blue Flax   *Linum lewisii*

FUMITORY FAMILY   Fumariaceae

Found mostly in Europe and Asia with only a few representative species in North America, this family is composed of annual, biennial, and perennial herbs that have divided, parsleylike leaves and unusual, irregular flowers. The flowers have two sepals, four united petals, and six stamens.

Golden Smoke   *Corydalis aurea*

The smokelike odor of this wildflower earned golden smoke its common name. It has bright yellow blossoms; weak, spreading stems, 4 to 24 inches tall; and pinnately compound, feathery, divided leaves. The irregular flowers have four petals united into a trumpet shape with two lips. The upper lip flares back into a spur. The flowers occur in erect clusters that are shorter than the leaves. It is the only species in Wyoming.

Golden smoke blooms in May and June and grows on gravelly hillsides and creek bottoms in the steppe and foothills from the Yukon to New Mexico.

Steer's Head   *Dicentra uniflora*

This plant has an unusual pink flower that is shaped like a steer's head: two petals flare out on each side and look like ears, and two lower, united petals resemble a nose. The plant has basal leaves divided into elliptical lobes. Steer's head is a spring bloomer, and its flowers appear just after the snow melts. This is the only species in Wyoming.

It grows in well-drained, gravelly, disturbed soils in the foothills, montane, and subalpine zones and only occurs in the Rocky Mountains in western Wyoming, eastern Utah, and eastern Idaho.

Golden Smoke *Corydalis aurea*

Steer's Head *Dicentra uniflora*

GENTIAN FAMILY   Gentianaceae

The gentian family is comprised of herbs; most of them grow in moist, cool habitats. Plants of this family have symmetrical flowers with four or five united petals and opposite leaves. There are over one thousand species distributed worldwide.

Prairie Gentian *Eustoma grandiflorum*

Prairie gentian's blue flowers are 1 to 2 inches wide, have five petals united at the base, and occur in clusters of two to six flowers per stem. Leaves are oval and opposite on stems that are 15 inches tall. It blooms from July to September. The habitat of this prairie wildflower is being destroyed by development, and it is now rare and endangered in Colorado. This is the only species in Wyoming.

Prairie gentian lives in moist meadows and grasslands in southeastern Wyoming and occurs in the Great Plains from Wyoming to New Mexico.

Green Gentian *Frasera speciosa*

Also known as *monument plant,* this tall, robust gentian grows up to 6 feet tall. The broad, elliptical, grayish green leaves grow 10 to 20 inches long and are arranged in whorls of four to six leaves. The greenish white flowers have four widely spread petals with purple basal spots. This hardy plant may grow for twenty years before flowering. Once it blooms, usually in June and July, it dies. This is the only species in Wyoming.

Green gentian is found on moist, grassy slopes in the foothills, montane, subalpine, and alpine zones and is widespread in the western United States.

Gentian *Gentiana*

Gentians can be seen blooming from late July into September, giving the meadows a last bit of color before fall. They have simple, opposite leaves with entire margins and flowers with five petals united at the base. The petal lobes flare and spread. Six species occur in Wyoming.

Gentians grow in wet soils in the foothills, montane, subalpine, and alpine zones.

The dark blue flowers of **Rocky Mountain pleated gentian (*Gentiana affinis*)** have united petals with lengthwise pleats. It has unbranched, leafy stems up to 12 inches tall with simple, opposite, oval leaves. It is widespread in the Rocky Mountains and grows in the foothills, montane, subalpine, and alpine zones.

Arctic gentian (*Gentiana algida*) has stemless flowers cradled in lance-shaped basal leaves. Petals are united nearly to the tips and are off-white or greenish with purple stripes. It occurs only in moist alpine zones in the Rocky Mountains from Montana to New Mexico.

Prairie Gentian *Eustoma grandiflorum*

Green Gentian *Frasera speciosa*

Rocky Mountain Pleated Gentian
Gentiana affinis

Arctic Gentian
Gentiana algida

Northern Gentian *Gentianella amarella*

This delicate plant, which grows 4 to 8 inches tall, has opposite, oval leaves and pink to lavender tubular flowers. The five petals are pointed and flare at the tips. It blooms in August and September. Three species of *Gentianella* occur in Wyoming.

Northern gentian grows in moist, sunny sites and is found in the foothills, montane, subalpine, and alpine zones and is widespread in western North America.

Rocky Mountain Fringed Gentian *Gentianopsis detonsa*

Masses of Rocky Mountain fringed gentian brighten high mountain meadows in August and early September. They have oval, opposite leaves and grow 6 to 12 inches tall. The showy, dark blue flowers have five fringed petals united into a tube with flaring tips. Rocky Mountain fringed gentian is common in the geyser basins of Yellowstone National Park and is the park's official wildflower. Three species occur in Wyoming.

Rocky Mountain fringed gentian grows in sunny, moist, boggy soils in the montane, subalpine, and alpine zones from Idaho and Montana to New Mexico.

Star Gentian *Swertia perennis*

Star gentian has single erect stems that grow 6 to 12 inches tall and have opposite, elliptical, entire leaves. The dark, purplish blue flowers have five sharply pointed petals with white veins on their undersides. The flowers grow in branched, open clusters along the upper part of the stems. Star gentian blooms from late July to September.

Star gentian is the only *Swertia* species in Wyoming and can be found in bogs and wet meadows in the montane, subalpine, and alpine zones from southern British Columbia and Alberta south through the Rocky Mountains.

Northern Gentian
Gentianella amarella

Rocky Mountain Fringed Gentian
Gentianopsis detonsa

Star Gentian   *Swertia perennis*

GERANIUM FAMILY   Geraniaceae

The geranium family has seven hundred species that occur mostly in the Northern Hemisphere. The annual or perennial herbs have compound or divided leaves and flowers with five petals and five sepals.

Wild Geranium   *Geranium*

Wild geraniums have branched stems and sharply pointed, palmately divided, alternate leaves. They grow in clumps with stems that grow 15 to 30 inches tall. These plants may feel sticky because they are often covered with glandular hair. The showy flowers, positioned well above the leaves, are comprised of five separate, rounded petals that often have pink or purple vein stripes. These lines, seen by insects, aid in pollination. Seven species occur in Wyoming.

Geraniums bloom from June to August and grow in dry to moist soils in all the vegetation zones.

Richardson's geranium *(Geranium richardsonii)* is a bushy, spreading plant with white flowers that are $^3/_4$ inch broad. The petals have light-purple stripes. Richardson's geranium grows in moist areas along streams in the foothills, montane, subalpine, and alpine zones and is widespread in western North America. It was named for John Richardson (1787–1865), a naturalist on John Franklin's 1819 arctic expedition.

Sticky geranium *(Geranium viscosissimum)* has light-pink, magenta, or reddish purple flowers up to $^3/_4$ inch across. Sticky geranium grows in dry, open, sunny sites and is found in the steppe, foothills, montane, and subalpine zones. It is widespread in the western United States. Early settlers and Native Americans used a poultice made from its leaves as a remedy for insect bites.

Sticky Geranium *Geranium viscosissimum*

Richardson's Geranium *Geranium richardsonii*

HEATH FAMILY   Ericaceae

Members of this family are usually woody perennials or shrubs. Leaves are simple, alternate or basal, often leathery, and evergreen. Some members lack green leaves. Flowers have four or five petals united into a cup or urn shape. The heath family is comprised of about 2,500 species that occur in temperate regions mostly in mature coniferous forests.

Bearberry   *Arctostaphylos uva-ursi*

Found in shady forests, bearberry grows in mats with woody stems that are 2 to 6 inches tall. It has rounded, glossy, alternate, evergreen leaves and small, urn-shaped, pink flowers with five, united petals. This plant is especially noticeable in the fall with bright red berries among its leaves. Bears are fond of the berries, and *arctos* and *ursi* both mean "bear." Some people call it *kinnikinnick,* which is derived from an Algonquin word meaning "that which is mixed." The dried leaves of bearberry and dried inner bark of red-osier dogwood *(Cornus sericea)* were mixed and used as tobacco. This is the only *Arctostaphylos* species in Wyoming.

Bearberry blooms in May and June. It grows in the montane, subalpine, and alpine zones and is widespread in western North America.

Prince's Pine   *Chimaphila umbellata*

Prince's pine, also known as *pipsissewa,* has a single woody stem. It grows 4 to 16 inches tall and has three to eight elliptical, shiny, evergreen leaves with small teeth on their margins. The saucer-shaped, nodding, pink flowers have five waxy petals and occur in erect clusters of two to eight flowers held well above the basal and lower stem leaves. Prince's pine blooms in July and August. High in vitamin C, the leaves are often used as tea and to flavor soft drinks. This is the only *Chimaphila* species in Wyoming.

Prince's pine grows in shaded, mature, coniferous forests in the foothills, montane, and subalpine zones and occurs from southern British Columbia and Alberta to Colorado.

Pinesap   *Hypopitys monotropa*

Pinesap is a saprophyte, which means it lives in conjunction with soil fungi called mycorrhizae that provide the plant with some of its nutrients. Because of this relationship, pinesap does not need chlorophyll to manufacture food. Since it doesn't photosynthesize, its leaves are reduced to small brown scales on pinkish orange, hairy, clustered stems that grow 2 to 12 inches tall. The urn-shaped, nodding flowers grow along the upper portion of each stem, which often droops at its tip when young and is erect when mature. It blooms in July and August. This is the only *Hypopitys* species in Wyoming.

Pinesap grows in conifer forests of the foothills, montane, and subalpine zones and is widespread in the western United States.

Bearberry fruit *Arctostaphylos uva-ursi*
Inset: Bearberry flowers

Prince's Pine
Chimaphila umbellata

Pinesap
Hypopitys monotropa

Bog Laurel   *Kalmia microphylla*
Often carpeting the edges of high mountain lakes, this woody, evergreen shrub grows 2 to 8 inches tall. Its leaves are opposite, oval, leathery, and glossy. The saucer-shaped, rose-colored flowers have five petals united at the base with the free ends forming shallow lobes. It blooms in June and July. Although many members of the heath family are used in herbal medicine, bog laurel contains poisonous alkaloids and should never be ingested. This is the only *Kalmia* species in Wyoming.

Bog laurel grows in moist to wet bogs and meadows along lakeshores and streambanks in the subalpine and alpine zones and is widespread in western North America.

Wood Nymph   *Moneses uniflora*
These dainty, inconspicuous, single-flowered forest dwellers are often overlooked. Wood nymphs are semiwoody perennials that have smooth, leathery, and rounded evergreen basal leaves with fine teeth on their margins. The erect, stiff, flower stalks grow 2 to 6 inches tall and have a single, white, nodding flower with five spreading, waxy petals and five yellow stamens. Blooming in July and August, this lovely, fragrant wildflower is also called *single delight, one-flowered wintergreen,* and *shy maiden*. It is the only *Moneses* species in the world.

Wood nymphs grow in the moist, deep shade of mature coniferous forests in the montane zone and are widespread in western North America.

Pink Mountain Heather   *Phyllodoce empetriformis*
Pink mountain heather is a low-growing, branched shrub with narrow, alternate, evergreen leaves. Masses of magenta, bell-shaped flowers grow in clusters at the stem tips. There are two *Phyllodoce* species in Wyoming, and they bloom from June to August.

Related to the heathers of the heath moors in Scotland, it grows in wet, boggy soils on lakeshores and stream edges in the subalpine and alpine zones in the northwestern Wyoming, southwestern Montana, and eastern Idaho; it occurs from Alaska south to Wyoming and Idaho and west to California.

Bog Laurel
Kalmia microphylla

Wood Nymph
Moneses uniflora

Pink Mountain Heather
Phyllodoce empetriformis

Woodland Pinedrops   *Pterospora andromedea*

Woodland pinedrops has tall, single, reddish brown stems with sticky hair. A saprophyte that lacks green chlorophyll, it lives with soil fungi called mycorrhizae that provide the plant with its nutrients. Since woodland pinedrops doesn't photosynthesize, its leaves are reduced to small, nongreen scales. Yellowish brown, urn-shaped flowers hang down and are spread along the stems. The stems grow 12 to 40 inches tall, become woody, and remain standing through the winter. It is the only *Pterospora* species in Wyoming.

Woodland pinedrops flowers in July and August and lives in dry, open forests in deep humus in the foothills and montane zones; it occurs from southern British Columbia and Alberta to New Mexico and Arizona.

Wintergreen   *Pyrola*

Wintergreens, often inhabitants of mature, old growth forests, have woody bases, leathery basal leaves, and erect flower stems. The simple, glossy leaves are evergreen and oval or elliptical. Their urn-shaped flowers have five united petals and grow on erect flower stalks with seven to twenty flowers per stalk. Five species occur in Wyoming.

Wintergreens generally bloom from June to August and grow in shady, moist woods and meadows. They are common and widespread in the western United States.

Pink wintergreen *(Pyrola asarifolia)* has shiny, round, basal leaves, 1 to 3 inches broad, and pink, cup-shaped flowers on leafless stems that grow up to 12 inches tall. It occurs in damp soils in shady sites in the foothills, montane, and subalpine zones.

Lesser wintergreen *(Pyrola minor)* has white flowers on stems 8 inches tall with basal leaves that are up to 1 inch across. The flowers are nodding, urn shaped, about $1/4$ inch deep, and characterized by a straight style protruding beyond the petals. It commonly occurs in montane forests.

Woodland Pinedrops
Pterospora andromedea

Pink Wintergreen
Pyrola asarifolia

Lesser Wintergreen   *Pyrola minor*

Grouse Whortleberry *Vaccinium scoparium*

Grouse whortleberry forms a dense ground cover over wide areas of pine forest. This erect shrub with green branches grows 12 inches tall. Oval leaves have fine teeth on their margins. The petite, pink, urn-shaped flowers have five united petals and hang under the leaves. Much sought after, its delicious reddish pink berries, and those of another species, highbush huckleberry *(Vaccinium membranaceum),* which has blue berries, are used for jelly and jam. They bloom in June and July. Five *Vaccinium* species grow in Wyoming.

Grouse whortleberry lives in cool, coniferous forests in the montane and subalpine zones in the central Rocky Mountains from southern British Columbia and Alberta to Colorado and Utah.

HONEYSUCKLE FAMILY   Caprifoliaceae

The honeysuckle family is comprised of shrubs with simple, opposite leaves and berrylike fruits. The flowers have five united sepals, five united petals, and five stamens. Many of the species have flowers attached to stems in pairs. Four hundred species of the honeysuckle family occur in the Northern Hemisphere in temperate and boreal regions.

Twinflower *Linnaea borealis*

An inhabitant of mature coniferous forests, this is a creeping, mat-forming plant with oval, evergreen leaves that are 1 inch long. Its white to pink paired flowers have five petals united in a narrow tube about $1/2$ inch long; they hang from the top of an erect stem that is 4 to 5 inches tall. It blooms in June and July. The genus *Linnaea* was named for Carolus Linnaeus (1707–1778), the father of the scientific naming system. This is the only *Linnaea* species in North America.

Some botanists place twinflower in the twinflower family (Linnaeaceae). It grows in moist soil in shady coniferous forests in the foothills, montane, and subalpine zones and is widespread in western North America.

Grouse Whortleberry fruit
Vaccinium scoparium

Grouse Whortleberry flowers

Twinflower
Linnaea borealis

Honeysuckle   *Lonicera*

Honeysuckles are woody shrubs that grow 24 to 72 inches tall and have opposite, elliptical leaves. The flowers have five, pointed petals that are united into a narrow, flaring tube. The hanging flowers are attached to the stem in pairs. Fruits can be shiny red or black depending on the species; six species occur in Wyoming.

Honeysuckles grow in moist, sunny to partially shaded woods in the foothills, montane, and subalpine zones. They bloom from May to July.

Black twinberry honeysuckle (*Lonicera involucrata*) is named for its pairs of black berries surrounded by a showy, red, leafy bract. The pale yellow flowers are surrounded by a green, leaflike bract. The berries are inedible and poisonous, unlike the edible and tasty red berries of Utah honeysuckle. Black twinberry honeysuckle occurs throughout Wyoming except in the Bighorn Range. It is widespread from Alaska to Arizona and New Mexico.

Utah Honeysuckle (*Lonicera utahensis*), also known as *red twinberry,* has cream-colored, paired flowers and pairs of red berries that are not surrounded by a leafy bract. Found in the Bighorn Range and in the mountains west of the Continental Divide in Wyoming, it occurs from British Columbia and Alberta to Utah and Colorado.

Black Twinberry Honeysuckle fruit   **Black Twinberry Honeysuckle flowers**
Lonicera involucrata

Utah Honeysuckle   *Lonicera utahensis*

Red Elderberry   *Sambucus racemosa*

Scattered through the mountains, this tall, spreading, woody shrub has opposite branches and pinnately compound leaves with five to seven leaflets. It grows up to 6 feet tall in favorable locations. Its small white flowers have five united petals; they occur in rounded or flat-topped clusters on the branch tops. Fruits are usually small red berries, but they may be blue or purple. There are three *Sambucus* species in Wyoming, flowering from May to July. All elderberries contain poisonous hydrocyanic acid, a cyanide compound. The berries should always be cooked before eating, as cooking reduces the poisonous compounds and renders them harmless. Some botanists place elderberry in the moschatel family (Adoxaceae).

Red elderberry grows in forest openings and moist areas along streams in the foothills and montane zones and is widespread in the western United States.

Snowberry   *Symphoricarpos*

These woody shrubs grow up to 24 inches tall and have grayish green, opposite leaves. The oval leaves have wavy margins and rounded tips. Snowberry flowers have five light-pink petals united in a flared tube. It is called snowberry for the clusters of white, waxy berries visible from late summer into winter.

Two species of snowberry can be found in the foothills and montane zones. They usually bloom in June and early July.

Western snowberry (*Symphoricarpos occidentalis*) has erect stems up to 30 inches tall. The leaves are elliptical and grow 3 inches long. Flowers often occur in pairs or are clustered at the branch tips. It grows in sunny sites near water in the foothills and low-elevation montane zones from the Great Plains to western Montana, Wyoming, Colorado, and Utah.

Mountain snowberry (*Symphoricarpos oreophilus*) is a low-growing, spreading plant that grows up to 36 inches tall. It has elliptical leaves that grow up to 1½ inches long. Tubular flowers, about twice as long as they are wide, hang in pairs or clusters under the leaves. It is found in the foothills, montane, and subalpine zones from southern British Columbia and Montana to California and New Mexico.

Red Elderberry
Sambucus racemosa

Western Snowberry
Symphoricarpos occidentalis

Mountain Snowberry   *Symphoricarpos oreophilus*

IRIS FAMILY   Iridaceae

Probably best known for the crocus (*Crocus* species) and bearded iris *(Iris germanica)* grown in home gardens, the iris family has 1,500 species worldwide. The flowers have three petal-like sepals, three petals, and three stamens. The sepals and petals may be similar in size and color.

Rocky Mountain Iris   *Iris missouriensis*

Rocky Mountain iris spreads by underground stems and may cover wide expanses of moist meadows. It has clusters of erect, strap-shaped basal leaves, 8 to 20 inches tall, that have stiff points. Pale to dark lavender flowers have three long, erect petals; three similarly colored, reflexed, petal-like sepals; and three stamens. One or two large flowers, 2 to 3 inches long, top the slender, naked, smooth stems. Looking somewhat like the cultivated iris of home gardens, this wildflower is easy to identify. It is the only species of iris in Wyoming. Its scientific name is derived from the Missouri River, where the Lewis and Clark Expedition first collected it in 1806.

Rocky Mountain iris blooms in May and June and is found in moist to wet areas (or places wet at least in the spring) in the plains, steppe, foothills, and montane zones. It is widespread and common in the western United States.

Blue-Eyed Grass   *Sisyrhinchium montanum*

You may not notice this grasslike wildflower among meadow plants until the glint of blue from the delicate flowers catches your eye. Its leaves are long, narrow, and flat with smooth margins; they grow 3 to 12 inches tall. The sky blue flowers have three petal-like sepals, three petals, and three yellow stamens in a prominent central eye. One to three flowers form flat-topped clusters on stems that grow up to 20 inches tall. It blooms in May and June. Four *Sisyrhinchium* species occur in Wyoming.

Blue-eyed grass grows in moist soils of meadows and grassy areas in the plains, steppe, foothills, and montane zones. It grows from northern Canada to Colorado.

Rocky Mountain Iris   *Iris missouriensis*

Blue-Eyed Grass   *Sisyrhinchium montanum*

LILY FAMILY   Liliaceae

The lily family has 4,200 species worldwide. Flowers have three sepals that are often petal-like, three petals, and six stamens. Leaves are simple with parallel veins. There are twenty-four genera and over thirty species in Wyoming.

Onion *Allium*

Onions have flat or round basal leaves. Tubular flowers have three petals, three petal-like sepals, and six stamens. The flowers are arranged in rounded clusters at the top of naked stalks. The plants have an onion odor and often resemble grasses when not in bloom. Wild onions are cousins of the garden onion. Since the leaves and bulbs of onions closely resemble the poisonous meadow death camas (*Zigadenus venenosus),* and they grow together, do not eat any bulb unless it has the characteristic onion odor. Seven onion species grow in Wyoming.

Some botanists place onions in the onion family (Alliaceae). Onions grow in dry or moist sites in all vegetation zones and are common in western North America.

Tapertip onion (*Allium acuminatum*) has two to four flat leaves and pink flowers on a 5- to 10-inch stalk. Its leaves are usually shorter than the flower stalk. Blooming in June and July, it grows in dry sites in the steppe, foothills, and montane zones mostly west of the Continental Divide from southern British Columbia to Arizona.

Shortstyle onion (*Allium brevistylum*) has two or more narrow, flat leaves, bright pink flowers, and stamens that are shorter than the petals. Flower clusters are held upright on stalks that grow up to 24 inches tall. It grows in wet meadows and along streambanks in the montane, subalpine, and alpine zones from central Montana through central Wyoming to eastern Utah and Colorado. Nodding onion (*Allium cernuum*) resembles shortstyle onion both in size and leaf shape; however, its flower cluster is conspicuously drooping rather than erect. Both occur in the same habitat and bloom in June and July.

Siberian chive (*Allium schoenoprasum*) has two hollow, round leaves and lavender-colored flowers on stalks that are 8 to 24 inches tall. It blooms in June and July and grows in wet meadows and along streambanks in all vegetation zones and occurs from Alaska to Colorado.

Prairie onion (*Allium textile*) has white flowers and two flat leaves, which are folded lengthwise and are as tall as the flower stalk. Blooming in May and June, this onion is very common, and it occurs in dry areas in the plains, steppe, and foothills from the Great Plains through Wyoming to southeastern Idaho and eastern Utah.

Tapertip Onion   *Allium acuminatum*

Shortstyle Onion   *Allium brevistylum*

Siberian Chive   *Allium schoenoprasum*

Prairie Onion   *Allium textile*

Sego Lily   *Calochortus nuttallii*

Sego lily, an unforgettable wildflower of dry habitats, has slender stems, which are 4 to 12 inches tall, and grasslike leaves. The solitary white flowers have three large petals with a purple, crescent-shaped spot at their bases and three pointed, greenish to whitish sepals. Also called *mariposa lily*, sego lily is the state flower of Utah. Native Americans and western pioneers ate its bulbs. Three *Calochortus* species occur in Wyoming.

    Some botanists place sego lily in the mariposa family (Calochortaceae). It blooms in June and July, grows in the plains, steppe, foothills, and montane zones, and is widespread across the western United States.

Glacier Lily   *Erythronium grandiflorum*

Glacier lily blooms at the edge of melting snowbanks in the high mountains, often carpeting large areas with yellow flowers. It has two smooth, lance-shaped basal leaves that grow 4 to 10 inches long. The flowers have three yellow petals, three yellow, reflexed petal-like sepals, and protruding stamens. One to five nodding flowers grow on each slender stalk. This is the only *Erythronium* species in Wyoming.

    Glacier lily blooms as early as May in the montane zone to late June in the alpine zone. It grows on moist, rich soil in partial shade in the montane, subalpine, and alpine zones. Although found from southern British Columbia and Alberta to Utah and Colorado, it is absent in Wyoming's Wind River Range.

Fritillary   *Fritillaria*

These captivating wildflowers grow 5 to 15 inches tall and have nodding, bell-like blossoms that are comprised of three petals and three petal-like sepals. They have smooth, elliptical leaves and smooth, slender stems. We have described both species found in Wyoming, leopard lily and yellow bells.

    Leopard lily and yellow bells occur in the plains, steppe, and montane zones.

    Leopard lily (*Fritillaria atropurpurea*), also called *checker lily,* has yellowish green petals and petal-like sepals, both spotted with brownish purple patches. Stems grow up to 15 inches tall and have narrow, pointed alternate leaves. Leopard lily blooms in May and June and grows in the foothills and montane zones of Idaho, Utah, Wyoming, Colorado, and New Mexico.

Sego Lily   *Calochortus nuttallii*

Leopard Lily   *Fritillaria atropurpurea*

Glacier Lily
Erythronium grandiflorum

Yellow bells (Fritillaria pudica) has solitary basal leaves and bright yellow flowers on stalks that grow up to 10 inches tall. The flowers turn reddish with age. It blooms early in the spring in April and May. Yellow bells grow in the plains, steppe, and foothills zones from southern Saskatchewan, Alberta, and British Columbia to Colorado and Utah.

Sand Lily   *Leucocrinum montanum*
Also called *star lily,* sand lily is stemless and has grasslike basal leaves and white flowers with three petal-like sepals and three petals. The flowers bloom in early spring, growing singly or in clusters from the center of the basal leaves.

Some botanists place sand lily in the spider-plant family (Anthericaceae). It is the only species in this genus. It grows in the dry plains, foothills, and lower elevations of the montane zone from Montana, South Dakota, and Nebraska to Colorado, Wyoming, and west to California.

Wood Lily   *Lilium philadelphicum*
The flowers of this large, showy, orange lily have three petal-like sepals and three petals with purple spots near their bases. The narrow leaves, in whorls of three to six, are arranged on stems that grow up to 24 inches tall. The flowers occur singly or occasionally in pairs on the tops of the stems. It blooms in June and July. This is the only *Lilium* species in Wyoming.

Wood lilies grow in moist, mixed woods and aspen stands from the plains and foothills to the lower montane zone from British Columbia, Alberta, and Saskatchewan to New Mexico and Arizona.

Common Alp Lily   *Lloydia serotina*
Common alp lily is a delicate plant with solitary flowers that bloom atop a single, leafy stem that grows 2 to 6 inches tall. It has narrow, grasslike basal leaves. The white flowers bloom in June and July and have three petals and three petal-like sepals with purplish veins and bases. This is the only alp lily species in North America.

This beautiful wildflower grows only on rocky slopes in the alpine zone in all of Wyoming's mountains except the Medicine Bow Range. It is widespread in western North America.

Yellow Bells *Fritillaria pudica*

Sand Lily *Leucocrinum montanum*

Wood Lily *Lilium philadelphicum*

Common Alp Lily *Lloydia serotina*

False Solomon's Seal   *Maianthemum*

False Solomon's seal, a plant of shady streamsides, has elliptical, parallel-veined leaves and grows up to 24 inches tall. Its white flowers have three petal-like sepals and three petals. It resembles Solomon's seal (*Polygonatum* species) of the eastern United States.

Some botanists place false Solomon's seal in the lily of the valley family (Convallariaceae). It grows in the foothills and montane zones. We described both species that occur in Wyoming.

False Solomon's seal (*Maianthemum racemosum*), growing up to 24 inches tall, has very small flowers massed in pyramid-shaped clusters that are 2 to 6 inches tall. The broad, oval to elliptical leaves are 3 to 8 inches long and have wavy margins. It blooms in June and July and occurs from British Columbia to Colorado.

Star false Solomon's seal (*Maianthemum stellatum*) has five to ten starlike flowers that are $1/2$ inch broad and occur in open clusters $1/2$ to 3 inches long. The elliptical, straight-edged leaves grow up to 5 inches long. This plant grows 6 to 12 inches tall. Blooming in May to July, it occurs from the Yukon to Colorado.

Fairy Bells   *Prosartes trachycarpa*

Fairy bells grows in shady woods and has greenish white, bell-shaped flowers that hang in pairs from 12- to 24-inch-tall leafy stems. Its alternate leaves are simple, and it blooms in May and June. Fuzzy orange berries ripen in late summer, are not poisonous, and have a slightly sweet taste. This is the only *Prosartes* species in Wyoming.

Some botanists place fairy bells, which was formerly called *Disporum trachycarpum,* in the mariposa family (Calochortaceae). It is found in the plains, foothills, montane, and subalpine zones from southern British Columbia and Alberta to New Mexico.

Twisted Stalk   *Streptopus amplexifolius*

Twisted stalk has opposite, oval leaves, up to 5 inches long, on a stem that appears to bend at each leaf attachment. Its cream-colored, bell-shaped flowers, each with a bent stalk, hang singly below a leaf. The flowers, sometimes hidden from view, bloom in June and July and are composed of three reflexed petals and three reflexed petal-like sepals. The flowers produce single, oval red berries in the late summer and fall. This is the only *Streptopus* species in Wyoming.

Some botanists place twisted stalk in the mariposa family (Calochortaceae). It grows in moist, shady areas in the montane zone and is widespread in western North America.

False Solomon's Seal
Maianthemum racemosum

Star False Solomon's Seal
Maianthemum stellatum

Fairy Bells   *Prosartes trachycarpa*

Twisted Stalk   *Streptopus amplexifolius*
Inset: Twisted Stalk fruit

Wild Hyacinth   *Triteleia grandiflora*

Wild hyacinth grows 8 to 24 inches tall and has flat basal leaves with a slight lengthwise fold; the leaves grow 10 to 20 inches long. Blooming in May to July, the light to dark blue flowers have three petal-like sepals and three petals united in a funnel shape that is $^3/_4$ inch long; they grow in flat-topped clusters. Wild hyacinth grows from bulblike underground stems that Native Americans ate. This is the only *Triteleia* species in Wyoming.

Now placed in the funnel lily family (Themidaceae) by some botanists, it is present in semi-dry soils in the steppe, foothills, and montane zones of the Teton Range in Wyoming and west into Idaho. It occurs from southern British Columbia and Alberta to Wyoming and Oregon.

Beargrass   *Xerophyllum tenax*

Showy beargrass has large clumps of flat, needlelike basal leaves. Flowers grow in rounded, clublike clusters at the ends of stems that grow 24 to 36 inches tall. Blooming in June and July, beargrass only produces flowers every three to ten years. This is the only *Xerophyllum* species in Wyoming.

Some botanists place beargrass in the bunch-flower family (Melanthiaceae). In Wyoming it grows only in the montane zone between Yellowstone and Grand Teton National Parks; it occurs from southeastern British Columbia to Idaho and northern Wyoming.

Death Camas   *Zigadenus*

Species of death camas have grasslike basal leaves and grow 8 to 32 inches tall. Their white or greenish flowers have three petal-like sepals and three petals with a yellow to greenish basal spot. All parts of these plants are poisonous. Three *Zigadenus* species occur in Wyoming.

Some botanists place species of death camas in the bunch-flower family (Melanthiaceae). They grow in all vegetation zones.

Mountain death camas (*Zigadenus elegans*) has white to greenish flowers, $^1/_2$ inch across, that bloom from June to August; they occur in an open, elongate cluster that grows up to 14 inches long. The strap-shaped basal leaves grow up to 10 inches long. It occurs in the foothills, montane, subalpine, and alpine zones and is widespread in western North America.

Meadow death camas (*Zigadenus venenosus*) has small, white to cream-colored flowers that are $^1/_4$ inch or less across; they occur in a crowded, compact, cylindrical cluster that grows up to 8 inches long. The narrow, strap-shaped basal leaves grow up to 10 inches long. It blooms from May to June and grows in the plains, steppe, and foothills from southern British Columbia and Alberta to Utah and Colorado.

Wild Hyacinth
Triteleia grandiflora

Beargrass
Xerophyllum tenax

Mountain Death Camas
Zigadenus elegans

Meadow Death Camas
Zigadenus venenosus

MADDER FAMILY   Rubiaceae

The madder family is economically important and includes species that provide coffee, quinine, and the natural red dye *madder*. Members of this family have simple, entire, opposite or whorled leaves and flowers with five sepals and five petals. It has 6,500, mostly tropical, species worldwide.

Northern Bedstraw   *Galium boreale*

Northern bedstraw has weak, rough stems that are square in cross section and grow 8 to 24 inches tall; they are topped with dense clusters of tiny white flowers, which are typical of the madder family. Leaves are narrow and pointed and are arranged in whorls of four around the stem. Early settlers used the sweet-smelling foliage of northern bedstraw as mattress filling, hence the common name. Its roots produce a natural red dye and the foliage may be used for tea. Northern bedstraw is related to the European madder *(Rubia tinctorum)*, a well-known dye plant. Northern bedstraw blooms from June to August. There are eight *Galium* species in Wyoming.

Northern bedstraw grows in a wide variety of dry and semimoist habitats in the plains, foothills, and montane zones throughout the western United States.

MALLOW FAMILY   Malvaceae

The mallow family has nearly 1,500 species found mostly in tropical climates worldwide. There are a few species in temperate North America. The flowers have five sepals, five separate petals, and many stamens united as a central column. Seeds separate into orangelike segments.

Mountain Hollyhock   *Iliamna rivularis*

Also known as *globemallow,* this tall wildflower, growing 20 to 60 inches tall, looks like a small version of the garden hollyhock *(Alcea rosea)*. The maple-shaped alternate leaves are divided into five to seven lobes. It has cup-shaped, white to pink flowers, 1 to 1¹/₂ inches across, that have five broadly rounded petals and numerous stamens united as a central column. It blooms from June to August. Mountain hollyhock seeds require heat for germination and are among the first plants to appear after fire.

Mountain hollyhock is the only *Iliamna* species in Wyoming. It grows in moist sites in the foothills, montane, and subalpine zones, often in disturbed areas and along trails, and is found mostly west of the Continental Divide; it occurs from southern British Columbia and Alberta to Colorado and Utah.

Top: Northern Bedstraw
Galium boreale

Bottom: Mountain Hollyhock
Iliamna rivularis

Checkermallow   *Sidalcea*

Tall and leafy checkermallows grow 18 to 36 inches tall. They have rounded basal leaves and alternate stem leaves with palmately divided, pointed lobes. The flowers, about 1 inch wide, have five spreading petals with a column of united stamens extending beyond the petals. Three species occur in Wyoming.

Checkermallows grow in wet soils in the foothills and montane zones and bloom in July and August. They occur from Wyoming to New Mexico, Nevada, and California.

White checkermallow (*Sidalcea candida*) has smooth, hairless foliage and white flowers about 1 inch across. The flowers grow crowded in erect clusters at the ends of stems.

Purple checkermallow (*Sidalcea neomexicana*) has hairy stems and leaves that are somewhat stiff and rough to the touch. It has rosy purple flowers, about 1 inch across, arranged in loose, erect clusters.

Scarlet Globemallow   *Sphaeralcea coccinea*

Sometimes called *cowboy's delight,* this wildflower grows 4 to 8 inches tall. The hairy, grayish green leaves are palmately divided into three to five narrow, pointed segments. The salmon to dark orange flowers have five petals slightly notched at the tips and many yellow stamens united as a central column. Two *Sphaeralcea* species occur in Wyoming.

Scarlet globemallow blooms from May to July and grows on dry, disturbed sites in the plains, steppe, and foothills from southern British Columbia, Alberta, and Saskatchewan to New Mexico.

White Checkermallow
Sidalcea candida

Purple Checkermallow
Sidalcea neomexicana

Scarlet Globemallow   *Sphaeralcea coccinea*

MILKWEED FAMILY Asclepiadaceae

The milkweed family is characterized by thick, milky juice and simple, entire leaves that are opposite or whorled. The flowers have five sepals, five united petals, and five hornlike appendages that grow between the petals and the stamens. Seeds with silken threads are produced in woody pods. Milkweeds emit a strong, sweet odor to attract insects. They occur worldwide in mostly tropical and subtropical climates.

Milkweed *Asclepias*

Milkweeds grow up to 48 inches tall and have opposite, slightly fleshy, oval leaves with a smooth surface and entire margins. Flowers occur in terminal, rounded clusters and have five united, reflexed petals. The hornlike projections stand upright and give the flowers a spiky appearance. Milkweeds produce woody pods full of brown seeds that have silky hair attached to them. The light seeds rely on air currents for dispersal. The pods persist on dry stems through the winter. Thirteen species occur in Wyoming.

Milkweeds grow in the plains, foothills, and montane zones.

Swamp milkweed *(Asclepias incarnata)* has narrow, elliptical leaves, 2 to 6 inches long, and rosy pink flowers that are up to $1/2$ inch across. It blooms from June to September and grows in wet, marshy areas in the plains of northern and eastern Wyoming. It is widespread in the Great Plains west to the foothills of the Rocky Mountains.

Showy milkweed *(Asclepias speciosa)* has broad, oval leaves with smooth, entire margins. The largest leaves may be 7 inches long, and they all have prominent, pinkish midveins. Light-pink flowers, up to 1 inch across, occur in large, dense, rounded clusters. It blooms during June and July and is a preferred food of the monarch butterfly. Showy milkweed grows in sandy and gravelly roadsides and other disturbed soils in the plains, steppe, and foothills and is widespread throughout the western United States.

Swamp Milkweed   *Asclepias incarnata*

Showy Milkweed   *Asclepias speciosa*

MINT FAMILY   Lamiaceae

The mint family is a large group of 3,200 species of aromatic herbs with opposite leaves, irregular flowers, and square stems that are square in cross section. Flowers have five united sepals and five united petals that form two lips. Members of the mint family are most abundant and diverse in the Mediterranean region but are found worldwide.

Nettleleaf Giant Hyssop   *Agastache urticifolia*
Like other members of the mint family, this plant has four-sided stems and opposite leaves. It grows 20 to 40 inches tall and can be found in extensive patches that sometimes blanket entire hillsides. The coarsely toothed leaves have a strong, somewhat unpleasant odor when crushed. Its small, rosy purple flowers are trumpet shaped and have four stamens that extend prominently beyond the petals. The flowers grow in dense cylindrical clusters. The leaves are often used as tea, and its seeds are edible. The spent flowers with ripe seeds provide ample winter seed for small songbirds. Two *Agastache* species grow in Wyoming.

Often the first plant to colonize an area after logging, nettleleaf giant hyssop blooms from June to August and grows in moist, sunny areas in the foothills, steppe, montane, and subalpine zones from southern British Columbia and Alberta to Utah and Colorado.

Wild Mint   *Mentha arvensis*
Wild mint has many branched, four-sided stems that grow 8 to 32 inches tall. The opposite leaves are oval and sharply toothed. Its irregular, pink to light-violet flowers have petals united in a short tube that is almost regular in shape; they are arranged in whorled clusters where leaves attach to the stem. All wild mints are edible, and oils of this and related species are used as flavorings in a variety of food and medicinal products. Crushing the leaves releases a typical mintlike odor. Two *Mentha* species occur in Wyoming.

Wild mint blooms in July and August and grows in moist soils along streams and rivers in the plains, steppe, and montane zones. It is widespread in North America.

Nettleleaf Giant Hyssop
Agastache urticifolia

Wild Mint
Mentha arvensis

Nettleleaf Giant Hyssop   *Agastache urticifolia*

Mintleaf Beebalm *Monarda fistulosa*

Mintleaf beebalm has unbranched, smooth stems that grow 12 to 24 inches tall. The oval or lance-shaped opposite leaves have coarse teeth along their margins. Its purple or rose, irregular flowers, about 1 inch long, have a narrow, erect upper lip and a wider, spreading, reflexed, lobed lower lip. These brightly colored flowers grow in round, terminal clusters and attract hummingbirds that feed on the nectar they produce. It blooms in July and August. There are cultivated varieties of mintleaf beebalm grown for the home garden. Wyoming is home to two native *Monarda* species.

Mintleaf beebalm grows in moist to semi-dry soils in the plains, steppe, and montane zones from southern British Columbia, Alberta, and Saskatchewan to Arizona and New Mexico.

Selfheal *Prunella vulgaris*

Although sometimes seen as a lawn weed, this native mint grows up to 12 inches tall in moist sites. Its pink flowers, about $^1/_2$ inch long, have a large, hooded upper lip and a short, reflexed lower lip with three lobes. The flowers grow in compact, cylindrical, terminal clusters that are 1 to 2 inches long. The opposite leaves are sparse. Selfheal is known for its use in herbal medicine, and this is the only *Prunella* species found in Wyoming.

Selfheal blooms from June to September and grows in open, partially shady sites in the foothills and montane zones. It is widespread in western North America.

Skullcap *Scutellaria galericulata*

Skullcap has four-sided, weak, slender stems that grow 4 to 32 inches tall. Its bluish purple flowers have a hooded upper lip and a broad, longer lower lip. The flowers occur in pairs in the leaf notches along the upper stem. There are two *Scutellaria* species in Wyoming. This wildflower has sedative properties and is used in herbal medicines.

Skullcap blooms from June to August and grows along river edges in the plains, steppe, and foothills throughout western North America.

Swamp Hedgenettle *Stachys palustris*

Growing in wet soils, swamp hedgenettle has sticky, hairy, four-sided stems that grow 8 to 32 inches tall. Its hairy leaves are opposite, oval, and toothed. The pinkish to dark purple flowers have a broad upper lip with a flared lower lip that has three lobes. They are arranged in whorls that occur near the top of tall stems.

Swamp hedgenettle, the only *Stachys* species in Wyoming, blooms from June to August and grows in open, moist areas in the plains, steppe, and foothills. It is widespread in the western United States.

Mintleaf Beebalm *Monarda fistulosa*

Selfheal *Prunella vulgaris*

Skullcap *Scutellaria galericulata*

Swamp Hedgenettle *Stachys palustris*

MUSTARD FAMILY   Brassicaceae

The mustard family is characterized by flowers with four sepals, four petals arranged in a cross shape, and six stamens. Some species are weedy plants and others important garden vegetables such as cabbage and broccoli (*Brassica* species) and watercress (*Nasturtium officinale*). The 3,200 species in this family occur throughout the cooler regions of the Northern Hemisphere. Many of the wildflowers in the mustard family are very similar in appearance. Botanists generally separate them by microscopic characteristics. The genera and species we illustrated here are a few examples of some common individuals you might see in Wyoming.

Heartleaf Bittercress   *Cardamine cordifolia*

Heartleaf bittercress grows 8 to 24 inches tall and has alternate leaves. The lower stem leaves are heart shaped, while those on the upper stem are triangular with wavy-edged lobes. The white flowers, grouped in showy, rounded clusters, are typical of the mustard family: they have four rounded, separate petals and six stamens. There are three other *Cardamine* species in Wyoming.

Heartleaf bittercress blooms in June and July and grows in moist to wet soils, in sun or partial shade, along streams in the montane zone. In Wyoming, this species only occurs in the Medicine Bow Range. They occur from southern British Columbia and Alberta to New Mexico.

Whitlowgrass   *Draba*

Over twenty species of whitlowgrass can be found in Wyoming. Whitlowgrass varies from cushiony, mat-forming tufts to slender, upright plants. Their leaves are alternate. All species have simple leaves and flowers with yellow petals.

Whitlowgrass occurs in open, sunny slopes in all vegetation zones.

Golden whitlowgrass (*Draba aurea*) grows up to 8 inches tall and has oval to elliptical leaves and flower clusters along and near the top of solitary stems. As the flowers open in succession from bottom to top, there may be narrow, podlike, mature fruits on the lower portion of the stem and open flowers above. Golden whitlowgrass blooms in June and July. It occurs in the montane, subalpine, and alpine zones and is widespread in western North America.

Few-seeded whitlowgrass (*Draba oligosperma*) is a compact, tufted mat that grows 3 to 4 inches tall. Leaves are narrow, up to $1/2$ inch long, lance shaped, and tightly packed along the stems. Flowers occur in clusters held above the leaves on short stems and bloom in March or April at lower elevations to July in the alpine zone. Few-seeded whitlowgrass can be found in the montane, subalpine, and alpine zones from the Yukon to southern Colorado.

Top left: Heartleaf Bittercress
Cardamine cordifolia

Top right: Golden Whitlowgrass
Draba aurea

Bottom: Few-Seeded Whitlowgrass
Draba oligosperma

Western Wallflower   *Erysimum asperum*

This showy wildflower has large, mustard yellow flowers and leafy stems that grow 8 to 24 inches tall, though sometimes taller. The narrow leaves grow both in a basal cluster and alternately on the stem. The flowers are $^1/_2$ inch across and have four oval petals in a cross shape with a prominent, protruding style. They are arranged in erect, rounded clusters on the top of single stems. Four *Erysimum* species occur in Wyoming and bloom from May to June.

Western wallflower grows in sandy, dry, open areas in all vegetation zones from southern Canada to New Mexico.

Alpine Bladderpod   *Lesquerella alpina*

Alpine bladderpod, a tufted, matlike plant with narrow, silvery basal leaves, blooms in early spring. Fruits produced after blooming are small, inflated, egg-shaped pods. Branched hairs, which can be seen only with magnification, cover the leaves. It has dense clusters of small yellow flowers that rise above the center of the leafy mat. Thirteen *Lesquerella* species grow in Wyoming.

Alpine bladderpod grows on dry slopes in the plains, steppe, montane, and subalpine zones from southern Alberta and Saskatchewan into Colorado and Utah.

Alpine Pennycress   *Noccaea montana*

Alpine pennycress is a slender, leafy plant that grows in clumps up to 10 inches tall. The basal leaves are rounded, while the alternate leaves on the stem are elliptical. Its white flowers have four petals and are arranged in terminal clusters. It blooms from May to July. Two *Noccaea* species occur in Wyoming.

Formerly called *Thlaspi montanum,* alpine pennycress occurs mostly west of the Continental Divide, but it does grow in the Medicine Bow Range. It grows in sunny areas or partial shade on moist hills and meadows in the foothills, montane, subalpine, and alpine zones from Montana to New Mexico.

Western Wallflower
Erysimum asperum

Alpine Bladderpod
Lesquerella alpina

Alpine Pennycress
Noccaea montana

Common Twinpod *Physaria didymocarpa*

This short, tufted plant grows up to 3 inches tall. The spoon-shaped leaves are hairy and grayish green and have a narrow petiole. The flowers have four yellow petals and occur in clusters on stems that grow 7 inches tall and rise from the outer edges of the leafy clump. It is known as common twinpod or *double bladderpod* for its small, swollen, egglike, mature fruits. It blooms in May and June. There are ten *Physaria* species in Wyoming.

Common twinpod grows on rocky ridges and dry slopes in the foothills, montane, subalpine, and alpine zones from southern British Columbia and Alberta to South Dakota, Wyoming, and Idaho.

Alpine False Candytuft *Smelowskia calycina*

Alpine false candytuft is a grayish green, tufted plant that grows 2 to 8 inches tall. The hairy basal leaves, up to 4 inches long, are pinnately divided into lobes with five to nine segments. The off-white flowers have four petals with a pinkish tinge on the backside and occur in terminal clusters. This is the only *Smelowskia* species that occurs in Wyoming.

Named for Timotheus Smelowsky, a Russian botanist from the 1700s, alpine false candytuft blooms in June and July and grows only on rocky, open sites in the subalpine and alpine zone. It is widespread in western North America.

Prince's Plume *Stanleya pinnata*

These tall, robust wildflowers have a woody base and grow up to 48 inches tall. Single, alternate leaves grow on waxy stems. The flowers have four yellow petals, four yellow sepals, and six stamens that extend beyond the petals; the flowers grow in tall, erect, feathery-looking clusters. This showy plant, often seen along roadsides blooming in June, grows in soils containing selenium. Plants growing on seleniferous soils are toxic to livestock. Three *Stanleya* species occur in Wyoming.

Prince's plume grows in the plains, steppe, and foothills and occurs throughout western North America.

Common Twinpod
Physaria didymocarpa

Alpine False Candytuft
Smelowskia calycina

Prince's Plume
Stanleya pinnata

NETTLE FAMILY   Urticaceae

The six hundred species of the nettle family are characterized by stinging hair and have small, inconspicuous flowers. Species of this family occur primarily in warmer, subtropical and tropical zones and are of little economic importance. Only one species occurs in Wyoming.

Stinging Nettle   *Urtica dioica*

This tall, coarse, leafy plant, with four-sided stems covered with stinging hair, grows 20 to 36 inches tall. The opposite leaves are lance shaped and have coarse teeth. Small green flowers grow in drooping clusters along the upper part of the stem. The plants resemble wild mint *(Mentha arvensis),* but stinging nettle flowers are green and occur in hanging clusters, unlike wild mint flowers, which are pinkish purple in erect clusters. The hair may cause itching and burning on contact, but the effects of a brush with stinging nettle, while unpleasant, are short term for most people. The leaves are often used as spring greens since the stinging hair is rendered harmless after cooking.

Stinging nettle blooms from June to August and grows in moist, boggy, and disturbed soils in the plains, steppe, foothills, and montane zones throughout western North America.

OLEASTER FAMILY   Elaeagnaceae

The thorny, woody shrubs of the oleaster family have inconspicuous flowers and showy berries. It is a small family of only fifty species.

Silver Buffaloberry   *Shepherdia argentea*

Silver buffaloberry is a large, woody shrub with thorny stems and opposite, silvery gray, round-tipped leaves. In favorable growing conditions it can grow 18 feet tall. Tiny, inconspicuous, brownish green flowers appear on naked branches in early spring before leaves emerge. Its bright scarlet, glossy, edible berries are difficult to pick from the thorny branches and are often shaken down onto a tarp for collection. Rich in vitamin C, the berries, once used as a food source by Native Americans and early settlers, are now used for jelly, wine, and catsup. Two *Shepherdia* species occur in Wyoming. The other, Canada buffaloberry *(Shepherdia canadensis),* differs by not having thorns.

Silver buffaloberry grows along streams and moist draws in the plains, steppe, and foothills from Alaska to New Mexico.

Stinging Nettle
Urtica dioica

Silver Buffaloberry fruit
Shepherdia argentea

Silver Buffaloberry flowers

ORCHID FAMILY   Orchidaceae

With over 450 genera and 15,000 species worldwide, the orchid family is one of the largest families of flowering plants. They are most abundant in the tropics. The leaves are simple and have parallel veins, and flowers are irregular with three petal-like sepals and three petals. Most often two of the petals and three of the sepals are alike, while the lower petal is modified into an inflated lip. There are twenty-six species of orchids in Wyoming.

Fairy Slipper Orchid   *Calypso bulbosa*
Fairy slipper, an exquisite orchid, has a single, egg-shaped basal leaf and a 2- to 5-inch flower stalk. The solitary, irregular flower has yellow hair at the base of a single, inflated lower lip, which is brownish pink and mottled purple. Above the lip spread five pink, narrow parts: two petals and three sepals. Fairy slipper orchid blooms in June and July. This orchid is in decline due to illegal collecting. If you find one in bloom, enjoy it in place but do not pick or dig it; it does not survive transplanting. This is the only species in this genus in the world.

Fairy slipper orchid grows in the deep, rich humus of mature spruce and lodgepole pine forests in the montane and subalpine zones from Canada to Colorado.

Spotted Coralroot   *Corallorhiza maculata*
Spotted coralroot has leafless, naked, reddish brown stems and grows 8 to 24 inches tall. The irregular flowers are attached along the upper stem; they are composed of three reddish, upper sepals, two reddish side petals with red spots, and an enlarged lower white lip with a wavy edge and purplish brown spots. Spotted coralroot is a saprophyte—lacks green chlorophyll—and obtains its nutrients through mycorrhizae, soil fungi associated with tree roots. Five *Corallorhiza* species grow in Wyoming, and they flower in June and July.

Spotted coralroot grows in moist to semi-dry, shaded soils in the foothills, montane, and subalpine zones. It is widespread in western North America.

Clustered Lady's Slipper   *Cypripedium fasciculatum*
A rare orchid, clustered lady's slipper has two oval leaves, 2 to 3 inches long, midway up the stem. A cluster of two to four brownish purple, irregular flowers grow at the top of the stem. The greenish brown flowers have two petals and three sepals, about 1 inch long, which are similar in shape, and a greenish yellow, inflated lower lip, which is ½ inch long. If you are fortunate to see this rare and endangered orchid, do not pick, dig, or disturb it in any way. It is the only lady's slipper in Wyoming, and it blooms in June and July.

Clustered lady's slipper is found in mature spruce forests of the montane zone in only a few locations in the Medicine Bow Range in Wyoming. It occurs in western North America from southern British Columbia to California and east to Wyoming and Colorado.

Fairy Slipper Orchid
Calypso bulbosa

Spotted Coralroot
Corallorhiza maculata

Clustered Lady's Slipper *Cypripedium fasciculatum*

Bog Orchid   *Platanthera dilatata*

Bog orchid grows in wet areas and may be recognized by its sweet, spicy fragrance. It has smooth, leafy, erect stems that grow 5 to 30 inches tall. Its alternate, lance-shaped leaves have sharp points and smooth margins. Irregular, whitish flowers are waxy; the upper sepal is modified as a hood, and there are two spreading sepals, two side petals, and a lower petal modified into a lip with a spur at its base. Dainty flowers, up to $1/2$ inch across, line the top of the stems. Seven *Platanthera* species occur in Wyoming.

Bog orchid blooms from June to August, grows in boggy, wet soils in the foothills, montane, subalpine, and alpine zones, and is widespread in western North America.

Hooded Ladies' Tresses   *Spiranthes romanzoffiana*

Another of the white-flowered orchids, hooded ladies' tresses grows 4 to 12 inches tall and has elongate, 2- to 4-inch-long basal leaves, which are narrow, elliptical, and have sharp points. The irregular flowers have greenish white sepals and petals that grow together and form a hood over a small lip. The flowers spiral around the upper portion of the stem. The flower cluster is thought to look like a braid of hair, hence the common name. Two *Spiranthes* species occur in Wyoming.

This orchid blooms in July and August and grows in moist meadows, streambanks, and wet areas in the foothills, montane, and subalpine zones. It is common in western North America.

Bog Orchid
Platanthera dilatata

Hooded Ladies' Tresses
Spiranthes romanzoffiana

PEA FAMILY   Fabaceae

This large, varied family is of great economic importance. Its species provide wood, food, dye, fiber, and chemicals. Leaves are alternate or basal and usually pinnately or palmately compound. Flowers have five united petals modified into specialized shapes. The upper petal, called the banner, is usually the largest. It is joined at the sides by two petals called wings, and below by two united petals called the keel. The fruits are pods with large seeds. There are 450 genera worldwide with about 12,000 species.

Milkvetch   *Astragalus*
Milkvetches are herbaceous plants with compound leaves, leafy stems, and flowers with a rounded keel. The keel is equal to or shorter than the banner. Milkvetches are easily confused with locoweeds (*Oxytropis* species). To identify them, use the general rule that milkvetches have leafy flower stems and a rounded keel with no beak, while locoweeds have basal leaves and a keel with a sharp beak. Milkvetch pods are often inflated and may be smooth to densely hairy. Over fifty-five species of milkvetch occur in Wyoming. We have included six common species to illustrate some of the variation within the genus. They bloom from late May to early August.

Milkvetches occur in dry, barren soils in all vegetation zones throughout western North America.

Field milkvetch (*Astragalus agrestis*) grows up to 12 inches tall and has pinnately compound leaves and reddish purple flowers in rounded, globelike clusters. It grows in moist soils in partly shady, disturbed sites and is found in the plains, foothills, and montane zones. It is widespread in the Rocky Mountains and the western Great Plains south to Nebraska and New Mexico.

Alpine milkvetch (*Astragalus alpinus*) forms mats with numerous, light-blue to pale violet flowers in an erect cluster. It grows up to 10 inches tall and is found in gravelly soils in the subalpine and alpine zones. It is widespread in the high mountains of western North America.

Two-grooved milkvetch (*Astragalus bisulcatus*) has hairy, pinnately compound leaves with seventeen to twenty-seven leaflets. It grows up to 24 inches tall. The reddish purple or purple flowers are grouped in dense clusters of twenty to thirty blooms on stems that are purple when mature. It grows in selenium-rich soils of the plains and steppe, accumulating selenium in its foliage, which imparts a strong skunklike odor. Two-grooved milkvetch occurs from southern British Columbia, Alberta, and Saskatchewan to Nevada, New Mexico, and Nebraska.

Field Milkvetch
Astragalus agrestis

Alpine Milkvetch
Astragalus alpinus

**Two-Grooved
Milkvetch**
Astragalus bisulcatus

Painted milkvetch *(Astragalus ceramicus)* grows 3 to 4 inches tall and has narrow, linear, grasslike leaves on short, branched stems. Its flowers are small and white to pale pink. The pods, inflated and almost round, have a red and white, multicolored surface that looks painted. It can be found growing in sandy soils, often on the edges of roads near the pavement, in the plains and steppe of central and eastern Wyoming from eastern Montana to western Nebraska and eastern Colorado.

Drummond's milkvetch *(Astragalus drummondii)* has whitish flowers on tall stems, which are 16 to 28 inches tall. The grayish green stems and leaves are covered with silky hair. Drummond's milkvetch has a leafy stem with elongate, cylindrical flower clusters. It blooms in June and July. Found in the plains, steppe, and foothills in the eastern half of Wyoming and western South Dakota, it occurs from southern British Columbia and Alberta to New Mexico and Utah.

Tufted milkvetch *(Astragalus sericoleucus)* is a low-growing, cushiony plant up to 3 inches tall. Two or three pinkish purple flowers grow on each stem and the compound leaves have three leaflets that are narrow and pointed. Tufted milkvetch grows on dry, barren hills in the plains and steppe. It blooms in May and early June. This species has a limited range, occurring only from south-western Montana through Wyoming to northeastern Utah and northwestern Colorado.

Painted Milkvetch fruit
Astragalus ceramicus

Drummond's Milkvetch
Astragalus drummondii

Tufted Milkvetch   *Astragalus sericoleucus*

Purple Prairie Clover   *Dalea purpurea*
This showy wildflower has many stems, 8 to 30 inches tall, that emerge in rounded clusters. The alternate leaves emit a strong, objectionable odor when bruised, and they are pinnately compound with seven to ten narrow, 2-inch-long leaflets. Its small, $1/4$-inch-long, bright pink flowers occur in densely packed, columnar clusters. The thick stem is covered with long, soft hair that remains after the flowers have finished blooming, giving it a conelike appearance. Six *Dalea* species occur in Wyoming.

Purple prairie clover blooms from June to August and grows on dry prairies and hills of the plains from southern Alberta and Saskatchewan to New Mexico and Texas.

Wild Licorice   *Glycyrrhiza lepidota*
Wild licorice has erect, sticky, reddish stems and grows 12 to 36 inches tall. The alternate leaves are pinnately compound with eleven to nineteen oval leaflets. Yellowish white flowers form compact, erect clusters. It is easily identified in the fall by its clusters of rust brown cockleburs. Native Americans used the roots of wild licorice as winter food and for medicinal purposes. It is not as strongly flavored as the European licorice *(Glycyrrhiza glabra)* that is used as flavoring for candy. This is the only *Glycyrrhiza* species in Wyoming.

Wild licorice blooms in June to August and grows as a weed in rich, somewhat moist soil, often along streams in the plains, foothills, and montane zones. It is widespread in the western United States and Canada.

Northern Sweetvetch   *Hedysarum boreale*
Northern sweetvetch grows as a leafy, rounded cluster of stems. It has showy, rosy pink or magenta flowers that droop slightly in erect clusters. These plants have gray, hairy stems and grow 6 to 24 inches tall. The pinnately compound leaves have alternate leaflets. Flowers have a keel that is rounded and longer than the banner and wings. They bloom from May to August. The distinctive pealike fruits of northern sweetvetch have indentations between the seeds and resemble a string of pearls. Four *Hedysarum* species grow in Wyoming.

Northern sweetvetch grows in dry, rocky soil, often along roadsides, in all vegetation zones throughout western North America.

Purple Prairie Clover   *Dalea purpurea*

Wild Licorice
Glycyrrhiza lepidota

Northern Sweetvetch
Hedysarum boreale

Showy Peavine   *Lathyrus polymorphus*

Showy peavine is an herbaceous perennial that has slender, partially upright or trailing leafy stems. It grows 6 to 12 inches tall. Its leaves are pinnately compound with four to eight pairs of leaflets. Showy flowers, 1 inch long with a magenta banner and light-pink keel, are arranged in clusters at tips of stems. This wildflower is related to the cultivated, perennial sweet pea *(Lathyrus latifolius),* which sometimes escapes from cultivation and grows wild as a weed. Showy peavine blooms in early May and June. Five *Lathyrus* species are native to Wyoming.

Showy peavine grows in dry, sandy soils of the plains zone from western South Dakota, western Nebraska, and eastern Wyoming to Texas.

Lupine   *Lupinus*

Lupines are annual or perennial wildflowers that grow in rounded clumps or tufts. They have palmately compound leaves with six to nine narrow, hairy, elliptical leaflets. Their blue to purple flowers form dense to sparse, erect flower clusters. There are seven species of this complex genus in Wyoming.

Lupines grow in dry, sunny, or shady sites in all vegetation zones.

Silvery lupine (Lupinus argenteus) has showy flowers in various shades of blue and silvery, hairy leaves with six to ten leaflets. Flowers are about ¹/₂ inch long with a prominent banner that is folded back lengthwise and a keel hidden within the wing. It grows 20 to 30 inches tall and blooms throughout the summer. Silvery lupine occurs in all vegetation zones and is widespread in the western United States.

Small lupine (Lupinus pusillus) is a low-growing plant with hairy basal leaves and short, 5- to 6-inch stems that are not much taller than the leaves. Bright blue flowers are ¹/₂ inch long and have a white or yellowish eye in the center. Mature pods have only two seeds. Small lupine blooms from May to August and grows in sandy soil and on sand dunes in the plains, steppe, and foothills from southern Saskatchewan and Alberta to New Mexico and Nevada.

Showy Peavine
Lathyrus polymorphus

Silvery Lupine
Lupinus argenteus

Small Lupine
Lupinus pusillus

Locoweed *Oxytropis*

Locoweeds have flowers in terminal, rounded clusters on mostly leafless stems. Their basal leaves are pinnately compound. Flowers have a definite beaked or sharply pointed keel, and they vary in color from white to pink to purple. Thirteen *Oxytropis* species occur in Wyoming and are easily confused with milkvetches (*Astragalus* species). In general, locoweeds have basal leaves, naked flower stems, and a beaked keel, while milkvetches have leafy flower stems and a rounded keel.

Locoweeds grow in dry, open sites in all vegetation zones.

Field locoweed *(Oxytropis campestris)* has light-yellow flowers with just a little purple on the keel. Clusters of three to fifteen flowers bloom from May to July; the flowers may be ³⁄₄ inch long. Leaves have seven to fifteen oval leaflets. Field locoweed grows up to 6 inches tall on rocky slopes in all vegetation zones from the Canadian Rockies south to northern Colorado and west to Utah and Oregon.

Nodding locoweed *(Oxytropis deflexa)* has light-violet flowers in rounded clusters and produces hanging pods. Pinnately compound leaves have nine to fourteen leaflets. It is an abundant, slender plant that blooms in sagebrush communities in May and early June and as late as August in subalpine zones. It can be found in the steppe, foothills, montane, and subalpine zones in the Rocky Mountains from the Yukon south to New Mexico.

Lambert's locoweed *(Oxytropis lambertii)* has a clump of silky basal leaves that surround erect, 10-inch stems of magenta to reddish purple flowers. It blooms from May to August and grows in dry sites in the plains, steppe, and foothills from Montana and Saskatchewan to Arizona and New Mexico.

Rocky Mountain locoweed *(Oxytropis sericea)* has white to pale yellow flowers that are 1 inch long and grow in compact, rounded clusters. The keel is tinged purple and has purple spots. Leaves have eleven to seventeen elliptical leaflets. It blooms from May to July. Rocky Mountain locoweed is a common plant of the steppe, foothills, and montane zones and is widespread in western North America.

Field Locoweed
Oxytropis campestris

Nodding Locoweed
Oxytropis deflexa

Lambert's Locoweed
Oxytropis lambertii

Rocky Mountain Locoweed
Oxytropis sericea

Lanceleaf Scurfpea   *Psoralidium lanceolatum*

Lanceleaf scurfpea is a short, spreading, leafy perennial that grows 6 to 12 inches tall. It has dark green, glandular-dotted, fleshy leaves that are palmately divided into three leaflets. Its inconspicuous, small, whitish flowers with a lavender keel are ¼ inch long and are clustered where the leaves attach to the stem. This plant is often found over large areas of the steppe since cattle do not eat it. It is also known to stabilize dunes. It blooms from June to August. Two *Psoralidium* species grow in Wyoming.

Lanceleaf scurfpea grows in loose sand or sandy soils in the plains and steppe from Saskatchewan to New Mexico and Texas, west to Washington, Oregon, and California.

Prairie Golden Banner   *Thermopsis rhombifolia*

Early in the spring in May and June, prairie golden banner blooms in bright displays with showy yellow flowers that are ½ to ¾ inch long and grow on erect stems. Ten to twenty flowers occupy each stem. It grows 6 to 16 inches tall, spreads by underground stems, and can occur in large patches. The alternate, hairy, grayish green leaves are palmately compound with three oval leaflets. Since most livestock do not graze prairie golden banner, it is widespread on otherwise overgrazed lands. Three *Thermopsis* species grow in Wyoming.

Prairie golden banner grows in dry, open sites, often along roadsides and in other disturbed areas, in the plains, steppe, montane, and subalpine zones from British Columbia and Alberta to Colorado and Utah.

Top: Lanceleaf Scurfpea
Psoralidium lanceolatum

Bottom:
Prairie Golden Banner
Thermopsis rhombifolia

Clover *Trifolium*

Clovers, related to the common plants found in lawns (*Trifolium* species), have palmately compound leaves with three oval leaflets. Small white or pink flowers are grouped in round clusters. There are eight native and six introduced species in Wyoming in all vegetation zones. They flower from May to August.

Long-stalked clover *(Trifolium longipes)* has round clusters of greenish white flowers that are $^1/_2$ inch long and occur at the top of 4- to 8-inch-tall leafless stalks. It has creeping stems that take root at intervals. It grows in moist soils in the foothills, montane, and subalpine zones from central Montana, Wyoming, and Colorado to Washington, Oregon, and northern California.

Parry's clover *(Trifolium parryi)* grows up to 4 inches tall in clumps or patches. It has reddish purple flowers densely arranged in round clusters on stems that are about 8 inches tall. It grows in moist sites of the subalpine and alpine zones from Montana to New Mexico.

Wild Vetch *Vicia americana*

This vinelike plant has bright magenta or violet flowers that are about 1 inch long and have a banner that is longer than the wings and keel. Two to nine irregular flowers are grouped in loose clusters along the stem where the leaves are attached. Weak trailing stems grow 8 to 48 inches long. The leaves are pinnately compound with eight to fourteen oblong leaflets. A tendril grows in place of the end leaflet. Flowering all summer long, the vines grow in grass and among other flowers. Three *Vicia* species grow in Wyoming.

Wild vetch grows in a variety of moist, sheltered habitats in the plains, steppe, foothills, and montane zones. It is widespread and common in the western United States.

ong-Stalked Clover   *Trifolium longipes*   Wild Vetch   *Vicia americana*

Parry's Clover   *Trifolium parryi*

PHLOX FAMILY   Polemoniaceae

The phlox family, found only in North America, has nearly three hundred species. They are most diverse and widespread in the western United States. Plants have showy flowers with five sepals and five petals that are united in a tube at their base and have lobes that flare and spread. The stigma of the flowers is divided at the tip into three lobes.

Skyrocket   *Ipomopsis aggregata*

Skyrocket, also called *trumpet flower* or *scarlet gilia,* has bright red flowers on slender stems that are 6 to 24 inches tall. The plant gives off a strong skunklike odor when crushed. Its leaves, pinnately divided into narrow leaflets, grow in basal rosettes and alternate on the stem. The flowers have five petals united into a trumpet-shaped tube that is 1 inch long. Seven species of this genus occur in Wyoming.

Skyrocket blooms from June to August and grows on dry, open sites in the foothills, montane, subalpine, and alpine zones throughout the Rocky Mountains and the western United States.

Phlox   *Phlox*

Phlox are compact plants that usually form large, rounded, matlike tufts. The narrow, opposite leaves are sharply pointed and grow close together on short stems. The flowers have five smooth, glossy petals united in a narrow tube with broad, flat, flaring lobes. Phlox bloom early in the season, in May and June at low elevations, to June and July in the alpine zone.

The twelve *Phlox* species in Wyoming grow in dry, open, often rocky sites in all vegetation zones.

Carpet phlox *(Phlox hoodii)* grows as a tufted mat and has woolly hair on its stems and leaves. Its tiny, narrow, stiff leaves are packed tightly along short stems. It has white to lavender flowers that are solitary at the ends of the stems. Sometimes called *Hood's phlox,* it was named in honor of Robert Hood, a member of the Franklin Expedition to the Canadian Arctic in 1819–1822. It grows in all vegetation zones and is widespread in western North America.

Longleaf phlox *(Phlox longifolia)* has pink flowers up to 1 inch long, narrow leaves up to 3 inches long, and upright stems that grow up to 10 inches tall. It does not form a dense mat but creeps along by underground stems. It grows in the plains, steppe, foothills, and montane zones from southern British Columbia and Montana south to New Mexico.

Rocky Mountain phlox *(Phlox multiflora)* grows as a large, loose, tufted mat. The leaves are narrow, somewhat stiff and pointed, and are 1¼ inches long. It has large white flowers, up to ¾ inch across, that seem to float above the leaves. It is found in semi-dry, open sites in all vegetation zones from Montana to Colorado.

Skyrocket   *Ipomopsis aggregata*

Carpet Phlox   *Phlox hoodii*

Longleaf Phlox   *Phlox longifolia*

Rocky Mountain Phlox   *Phlox multiflora*

Polemonium *Polemonium*

These wildflowers are beautiful, showy favorites of many travelers to the high country. They are herbaceous, leafy, sticky to the touch, and grow up to 24 inches tall. The leaves are pinnately compound. The funnel-shaped, showy flowers, either white or blue, have five united petals with flaring lobes and cluster at the tips of branches. All species have an objectionable, skunklike odor that is most noticeable when the plants are crushed. Six *Polemonium* species occur in Wyoming.

They bloom from June to August and grow in moist soils in the montane, subalpine, and alpine zones.

Leafy Jacob's ladder *(Polemonium foliosissimum)* is a large, leafy plant, 36 inches tall, with white flowers about 1 inch across. Compound leaves have leaflets up to 1 inch long. It grows in moist meadows near lakes or streams in the montane and subalpine zones in far western and southern Wyoming to Arizona and New Mexico.

Western Jacob's ladder *(Polemonium occidentale)* has bright blue flowers with yellow stamens visible in the flower tube and a three-lobed style that protrudes from the tube. It grows about 18 inches tall, and the stems are sparsely leafy. Western Jacob's ladder can be found in moist meadows in the montane, subalpine, and alpine zones and is common from northern Canada to Colorado.

Sky pilot *(Polemonium viscosum)* has sky blue flowers with a yellow center. They occur in showy, terminal, erect clusters on stems that grow up to 12 inches tall. It has basal leaves up to 6 inches long that have tiny, crowded leaflets. Sometimes sky pilots with white flowers grow among sky pilots with blue flowers. Sky pilot occurs in rocky sites in the subalpine and alpine zones from southern Alberta to New Mexico.

Leafy Jacob's Ladder
Polemonium foliosissimum

Western Jacob's Ladder
Polemonium occidentale

Sky Pilot *Polemonium viscosum*

Sky Pilot (white flowered)

PINK FAMILY   Caryophyllaceae

The pink family is comprised of annual and perennial herbs that have opposite leaves. The flowers have five petals that are often divided or notched on the ends. This large family is found in the Northern Hemisphere in cool climates.

Field Chickweed   *Cerastium arvense*
This smooth, slender plant grows 2 to 12 inches tall and has upright or slightly trailing stems. It has narrow opposite leaves and numerous branches that arise where the leaves are attached to the stem. Flowers have five separate, white petals that are deeply notched at the tip, giving them a two-lobed appearance. Field chickweed is a perennial and may become an unwelcome intruder in lawns. Seven *Cerastium* species grow in Wyoming.

Field chickweed blooms from May to August and can be found in dry, rocky sites in the foothills, montane, subalpine, and alpine zones throughout western North America.

Desert Sandwort   *Eremogone*
These low-growing, mat-forming wildflowers grow up to 12 inches tall. Their linear, opposite, grasslike leaves come to a sharp, almost spiny point. The flowers have five separate white petals in rounded, terminal flower clusters.

The five species in Wyoming can be found in dry, rocky hills and slopes in all vegetation zones. They were formerly considered part of the genus *Arenaria*.

Ballhead sandwort (*Eremogone congesta*) has a small, round, compact flower cluster on a slender stem that grows up to 8 inches tall. Ballhead sandwort blooms June through July. Quite common, it grows on dry, open slopes in the steppe, montane, subalpine, and alpine zones from southern Alberta to Colorado.

Hooker's sandwort (*Eremogone hookeri*) forms a leafy, prickly mat, and its clusters of flowers rise 2 to 3 inches above it. The opposite leaves have sharp, spiny tips. Although the plants resemble phlox, their dull white flowers have thinner petals that appear almost translucent. It was named in honor of Sir Joseph Hooker, an English botanist who collected plants in the Rockies in 1877.

Hooker's sandwort blooms in May and June and grows on sandy, gravelly hills and ledges in the plains and steppe from eastern Wyoming and southwestern South Dakota to Colorado and Utah.

Top left: Field Chickweed
Cerastium arvense

Top right: Ballhead Sandwort
Eremogone congesta

Bottom: Hooker's Sandwort
Eremogone hookeri

Arctic Sandwort *Minuartia obtusiloba*

Growing as a dense, mosslike, leafy mat, the stems of arctic sandwort grow only a few inches high and are crowded with short, linear, opposite leaves. The small flowers, nestled in the mat, have five separate, white petals that are notched at the tips and have green stripes. A central eye of showy yellow stamens highlights these flowers. Five *Minuartia* species occur in Wyoming. They were formerly considered part of the genus *Arenaria*.

Arctic sandwort grows only on dry, rocky slopes and ridges in the alpine zone and blooms in June and July. It is widespread in western North America.

Moss Campion *Silene acaulis*

Moss campion, a favorite flower of hikers in the highest mountain areas, grows as a mosslike, tufted mat that is blanketed with pink to rosy purple flowers. The mat grows 2 to 6 inches tall and has small, narrow, crowded leaves. The tubular flowers are ¹/₂ inch across and the tips of the petals flare out in five lobes. Nineteen *Silene* species occur in Wyoming.

Moss campion blooms in June and July and grows in sunny, somewhat moist soils in the alpine zone from Alaska to New Mexico.

POPPY FAMILY   Papaveraceae

Occurring mostly in cool temperate zones of western North America, the poppy family has nearly two hundred species. Species of this family have showy flowers of four to six petals and numerous stamens. They all produce a characteristic colored juice.

Rough Prickly Poppy   *Argemone hispida*

Blooming on the dry plains in June and July, rough prickly poppy has large, showy, white flowers. Its stem and divided, wavy edged leaves are covered with short spines. When cut, this plant oozes a sticky, white juice while the other species that occurs in Wyoming, crested prickly poppy *(Argemone polyanthemos),* oozes yellow juice. The flowers are about 3 inches across and have six petals and numerous yellow stamens. The stigmas are fused into a purple disk that is prominent in the center of the stamens. This spiny plant contains poisonous alkaloids in its tissues and is never grazed by livestock.

Prickly poppy grows in the plains of eastern Wyoming south along the foothills of the Rocky Mountains to eastern Colorado and eastern New Mexico.

**Arctic
Sandwort
*Minuartia
obtusiloba***

**Moss Campion
*Silene acaulis***

**Rough
Prickly Poppy
*Argemone
hispida***

PRIMROSE FAMILY   Primulaceae

Members of the primrose family are found mostly in cooler regions of the Northern Hemisphere. The eight hundred species of this family are leafy herbs with erect flower stalks. The showy, pink to white flowers of primrose family species have five united sepals, five united petals, and five stamens. Leaves are simple.

Northern Rock Jasmine   *Androsace septentrionalis*

This tiny, herbaceous annual has short, narrow basal leaves and three to twenty slender flower stalks that grow $1/2$ to 2 inches tall. Dainty white flowers in delicate, branched, flat-topped clusters have five petals and smell of jasmine. These plants look like tiny candlesticks and are sometimes called *northern fairy candelabra*. Four *Androsace* species occur in Wyoming.

Northern rock jasmine blooms from June to August and grows in moist, rocky soils in all vegetation zones. It is widespread in western North America.

Pretty Shooting Star   *Dodecatheon pulchellum*

Pretty shooting star has basal leaves and uncommon, bright pink flowers on leafless stalks that are 5 to 6 inches tall. The spoon-shaped to elliptical leaves have entire margins and grow up to 8 inches long. The flowers have five united petals that curve back and away from a projecting cone of united stamens that has a yellow collar and a point of purple anthers. The flowers occur in groups of three to ten. The unusual shape of these wildflowers is an adaptation to pollination. Bumblebees shake pollen loose with the vibrations of their wingbeats. There are three *Dodecatheon* species in Wyoming.

Pretty shooting star blooms in May and June and occurs on dry to wet sites in all vegetation zones throughout western North America.

Parry's Primrose   *Primula parryi*

This showy, robust plant, which grows up to 24 inches tall, has an unpleasant, skunklike odor. Its yellowish green basal leaves are large, up to 12 inches long, and elliptical to lance shaped. The bright magenta flowers, up to 1 inch across, have five broad, united petals; three to fifteen flowers occur in a terminal cluster on an unbranched stalk. Three *Primula* species occur in Wyoming.

Common to Wyoming's high mountains, Parry's primrose blooms in July and August. It grows along streams or on wet, rocky slopes only in the subalpine and alpine zones from Idaho and Montana to New Mexico.

Northern Rock Jasmine   *Androsace septentrionalis*

Pretty Shooting Star
Dodecatheon pulchellum

Parry's Primrose
Primula parryi

PURSLANE FAMILY   Portulacaceae

The purslane family has nearly six hundred species that occur primarily in the Western Hemisphere. Fifteen species occur in Wyoming. The plants have succulent leaves and flowers with two to many sepals; five or more delicate, thin, separate petals; and usually many stamens.

Lanceleaf Spring Beauty   *Claytonia lanceolata*

A real spring beauty, this wildflower grows 2 to 8 inches tall and often covers large areas of forest margins, blooming soon after snow has melted. It has three narrow, fleshy leaves: two opposite leaves on the stem and a single leaf at its base. Flowers have five white to pink petals, often with pink-striped veins, and two sepals. The petals are notched at their ends. Six *Claytonia* species occur in Wyoming.

Lanceleaf spring beauty grows in moist, open soil in the foothills, montane, subalpine, and alpine zones throughout western North America.

Bitterroot   *Lewisia*

These perennial plants, 1½ to 4 inches tall, grow from thick roots and have fleshy basal leaves. The solitary flowers occur on short stems and have many rose-colored petals. The genus was named in honor of Meriwether Lewis of the Lewis and Clark Expedition, who first collected this plant for science in Montana in 1806. Three *Lewisia* species occur in Wyoming.

Bitterroots grow in dry, gravelly, open sites of the steppe, montane, subalpine, and alpine zones.

Pygmy bitterroot (*Lewisia pygmaea*) has small flowers, up to ¾ inch across, with six to eight petals and two sepals. The flat leaves are 2 to 6 inches long and are taller than the flowers. Pygmy bitterroot blooms in June and July and occurs on dry slopes in the montane, subalpine, and alpine zones; it is widespread in the western United States.

Bitterroot (*Lewisia rediviva*) has five to seven fleshy leaves that are round in cross section and grow up to 2 inches long; they sometimes dry and disappear before the flowers open and are never taller than the flowers. The large flowers have twelve to eighteen rosy pink petals and six to nine pinkish sepals. Striking and showy, it is the state flower of Montana. The roots were a staple food for Native Americans. Although the roots are bitter, their taste improves after cooking. Bitterroot blooms in May and June and grows in the foothills, montane, and subalpine zones; it is widespread in western North America.

**Lanceleaf
Spring Beauty**
*Claytonia
lanceolata*

Pygmy Bitterroot
Lewisia pygmaea

Bitterroot
Lewisia rediviva

ROSE FAMILY   Rosaceae

The rose family, most commonly seen in the temperate regions of the Northern Hemisphere, has three thousand species worldwide. The flowers have five sepals, five petals, usually more than ten stamens, and one to many pistils. The leaves have small leaflike stipules at the base of their stems. Many of these annual and perennial herbs, shrubs, and trees grow economically important fruits and are used as ornamental plants such as apple (*Malus* species), cherry and peach (*Prunus* species), and rose (*Rosa* species).

Saskatoon Serviceberry   *Amelanchier alnifolia*
This woody shrub with reddish brown bark grows up to 12 feet tall. The leaves are simple and oval; from midleaf to tip they have teeth on their margins. The white flowers have five petals and occur in clusters near the branch tips. Early settlers used its blue berries for pies, and people still use the berries for jelly. Two *Amelanchier* species grow in Wyoming.

Saskatoon serviceberry blooms in May and June. It grows in moist or semi-dry soils on hillsides and streambanks in the plains, steppe, foothills, and montane zones from Alaska and the Yukon to Colorado and northern Arizona.

Alderleaf Mountain Mahogany   *Cercocarpus montanus*
Alderleaf mountain mahogany has smooth, grayish brown bark and grows up to 6 feet tall. The leaves are oval and have rounded teeth on their upper half. Flowers have five off-white, petal-like sepals arranged in a wide bell shape with protruding stamens. Its fruit has a dry, feathery plume attached. The other Wyoming species, cutleaf mountain mahogany (*Cercocarpus ledifolius*), has entire leaves with margins that roll under. It is usually found in central and western Wyoming. These are fire resistant shrubs that sprout from a burned base after a fire. Early settlers called them mountain mahogany for the dark wood.

Alderleaf mountain mahogany blooms from May to July and grows on slopes and in draws in the plains, foothills, and montane zones from Montana to New Mexico.

Black Hawthorn   *Crataegus douglasii*
Black hawthorn is a tall, woody shrub or small tree with rough, scaly, gray bark and straight thorns; it grows singly or in 3- to 12-foot-tall thickets. Its elliptical leaves are slightly glossy and sharply toothed. The saucer-shaped white flowers have five rounded petals and grow in flat-topped clusters. These lovely flowers, which bloom in June, have an unpleasant scent. Fruits are dark red, $^{1}/_{2}$ inch across, and resemble tiny apples. Although not tasty, they are not poisonous and provide abundant winter food for birds and small animals. Five *Crataegus* species occur in Wyoming.

Black hawthorn grows in well-drained soils near streams in the plains and foothills from southern British Columbia and Alberta to Arizona and New Mexico.

Saskatoon Serviceberry
Amelanchier alnifolia

Alderleaf Mountain Mahogany
Cercocarpus montanus

Black Hawthorn *Crataegus douglasii*

Mountain Avens *Dryas octopetala*

This beautiful plant of high alpine zones blooms soon after the snow melts. The showy, solitary, saucer-shaped flowers have eight to ten sepals and eight white petals that surround a cluster of yellow stamens. The flowers, up to 1 inch across, have short stems and are nestled in mats of leathery, elliptical leaves with round teeth on their margins. This is the only *Dryas* species in Wyoming.

Mountain avens is found on rocky, open slopes in the subalpine and alpine zones in the western and northern mountains of Wyoming; it occurs from Alaska to Colorado and Utah.

Wild Strawberry *Fragaria virginiana*

Wild strawberry spreads by runners and grows 1½ to 6 inches tall. Its palmately compound basal leaves have three, toothed, oval leaflets. The white, saucer-shaped flowers have five broad petals that grow up to 1 inch across. It is related to the cultivated strawberry (*Fragaria* species) and the small, red, tasty fruits are a real treat to snack on in the wild. Two *Fragaria* species occur in Wyoming.

Wild strawberry blooms from May to July and grows in semi-dry to moist sunny sites in all vegetation zones and is widespread in the western United States.

Avens *Geum*

These wildflowers have pinnately compound leaves and flowers with five broad petals. Leaves have a large terminal lobe with lateral lobes that become smaller toward the base. There are six species in Wyoming.

Found in all vegetations zones, avens are widespread throughout western North America.

Alpine avens (Geum rossii) is a short, leafy plant that grows 4 to 8 inches tall. The single yellow flowers have five petals. Alpine avens and cinquefoil (*Potentilla* species) look alike and may be easily confused. Alpine avens has basal leaves and a cone-shaped or cup-shaped flower base where the petals are attached. Cinquefoil has a nearly flat flower base and leafy stems.

Alpine avens blooms from June to July and grows in rocky meadows and on slopes in the subalpine and alpine zones. It is widespread in western North America.

Old man's whiskers (Geum triflorum), also called *avens, prairie smoke,* and *prairie plume,* has hairy foliage and grows 4 to 12 inches tall. Its flowers have reddish purple, reflexed sepals and reddish or yellowish petals that form an urn-shaped flower. Three flowers occur in each nodding terminal cluster. Seeds are attached to long plumes, which allow wind to carry them.

Old man's whiskers blooms from May to July. It grows on moist slopes and meadows often in gravelly soils in all vegetation zones throughout western North America.

Mountain Avens   *Dryas octopetala*

Wild Strawberry   *Fragaria virginiana*

Alpine Avens   *Geum rossii*

Old Man's Whiskers   *Geum triflorum*

Mountainspray   *Holodiscus dumosus*

Mountainspray is a woody shrub that grows up to 5 feet tall. It has small, wedge-shaped leaves with rounded teeth from the center of the leaf to its tip. Tiny whitish flowers occur along the branch tips in dense clusters that are 2 to 4 inches long. The individual flowers, which have typical rose family characteristics, are too small to observe in detail. The shrub blooms in July and is covered with these delicate floral sprays, hence its common name. This is the only *Holodiscus* species in Wyoming.

Mountainspray grows in sun or shade, among rocks and along river drainages in the foothills and montane zones. It can be found in west and central Wyoming and central Idaho to Utah and Arizona.

Alpine Ivesia   *Ivesia gordonii*

Alpine ivesia, also called *Gordon's ivesia,* is a low-growing, tufted plant that grows 4 to 8 inches tall. It has hairy, pinnately compound basal leaves with ten to twenty small, overlapping leaflets. Each leaflet is deeply divided into two to five narrow lobes. The flowers have five yellowish green sepals and five yellow petals; the sepals are longer than the petals. Flowers grow in dense clusters on nearly naked stems. It is named for Joseph Ives, explorer and army officer, and for George Gordon, who first collected the plant in 1844. This is the only *Ivesia* species in Wyoming.

Alpine ivesia blooms in June and July and grows among sagebrush and in grassy, rocky soils in the montane, subalpine, and alpine zones; it occurs in Idaho and Montana to Colorado and Utah.

Shrubby Cinquefoil   *Pentaphylloides floribunda*

Shrubby cinquefoil grows 12 to 36 inches tall and has woody stems with shredding, reddish brown bark. Its pinnately compound leaves have five leaflets covered with silky white hair. One to seven bright yellow flowers, up to 1 inch across, have five broad petals and grow in clusters at the tops of the branches. This shrub is showy during June, July, and August when in bloom and is cultivated and used as an ornamental plant. It is the only *Pentaphylloides* species in Wyoming.

Shrubby cinquefoil, formerly known as *Potentilla fruticosa,* grows in moist to dry, rocky sites in all vegetation zones and is widespread in western North America.

Mountainspray
Holodiscus
dumosus

Alpine Ivesia
Ivesia gordonii

Shrubby
Cinquefoil
Pentaphylloides
floribunda

Cinquefoil *Potentilla*

Cinquefoils, commonly seen in Wyoming, have palmately or pinnately compound leaves and pretty, saucer-shaped flowers with five broad, rounded, off-white, cream, or yellow petals. The flowers grow in flat-topped clusters. The base of the flower, where the petals and sepals are attached, is flat. There are twenty-seven *Potentilla* species in Wyoming.

Cinquefoils grow in various habitats from dry to moist sites in all vegetation zones in the western United States. Since they withstand heavy grazing, they are often seen in overgrazed areas.

Silverweed cinquefoil *(Potentilla anserina)* is matlike and spreads by runners; it has bright yellow flowers that are nearly 1 inch across. The densely hairy, pinnately compound, silvery gray leaves have eleven to twenty-five coarsely toothed leaflets. Blooming from May to June, it grows in moist sites along rivers and on disturbed soil in the plains, steppe, foothills, and montane zones. It is widespread in western North America.

White cinquefoil *(Potentilla arguta)* grows 16 to 32 inches tall and has glandular hair on its foliage, making it sticky to the touch. Its flowers are whitish to cream colored. The leaves are pinnately divided into seven to eleven coarsely toothed leaflets. White cinquefoil blooms in June and July. It grows on dry, disturbed soils in meadows and open woods in the plains, steppe, foothills, and montane zones from southern British Columbia and Alberta to New Mexico. Sticky cinquefoil *(Potentilla glandulosa)* resembles white cinquefoil but is a little smaller. It is also common and grows in the montane, subalpine, and alpine zones from southern British Columbia and Alberta to Colorado.

Mountain meadow cinquefoil *(Potentilla diversifolia)* grows up to 10 inches tall and has palmately compound, mostly basal, leaves with five to seven leaflets. The leaves are bluish green and the leaflets are lance shaped with toothed margins. It has many bright yellow flowers in open clusters that sway on the ends of slender stems. Blooming in June and July, it occurs in the foothills, montane, subalpine, and alpine zones from southern British Columbia and Alberta to Arizona and New Mexico.

Silverweed Cinquefoil *Potentilla anserina*

White Cinquefoil
Potentilla arguta

Mountain Meadow Cinquefoil
Potentilla diversifolia

Common Chokecherry   *Prunus virginiana*

Common chokecherry is a woody shrub that grows 6 to 24 feet tall and has oval, pointed leaves that have fine teeth on their margins. Its small flowers have five whitish, rounded petals that occur in bottlebrush-shaped clusters. Dark purple berries hang in heavy bunches in the fall. Native Americans and early settlers used them in pemmican and syrup. They remain popular today in jellies, syrups, and wines. The seeds and leaves should not be eaten as they contain hydrocyanic acid, a poisonous compound. Six *Prunus* species occur in Wyoming.

Common chokecherry usually blooms in May and June and grows in moist, open areas along streams in the plains, steppe, foothills, and montane zones throughout western North America.

Antelope Bitterbrush   *Purshia tridentata*

Antelope bitterbrush is a short, woody, spreading shrub that grows up to 24 inches tall. The small, wedge-shaped leaves have three lobes at their tips and are green on top and covered with white hair underneath. The flowers have five yellow petals and a sweet, strong fragrance. It is known as bitterbrush because the oils in the leaves, fruits, and stems are very bitter. This is the only *Purshia* species in Wyoming.

Antelope bitterbrush is an important browse plant for deer and antelope and is common in dry sites in the steppe and foothills throughout the western United States.

Wild Rose   *Rosa sayi*

Wild rose, known for its large, rose-colored flowers, has prickly spines on its stems and grows 3 to 6 feet tall. Its leaves are pinnately compound and have five to seven sharply toothed leaflets. The saucer-shaped flowers have five rounded petals, many yellow stamens, and are very fragrant. The fruits, called *rose hips,* are reddish orange, fleshy, packed with seeds, and high in vitamin C. There are five *Rosa* species in Wyoming.

Wild rose blooms from May to July and grows in open or wooded, moist soils along streams in the plains, steppe, foothills, and montane zones. It is widespread in North America.

Top left: Common Chokecherry flowers
Prunus virginiana
Inset: Common Chokecherry fruit

Top right: Antelope Bitterbrush
Purshia tridentata

Wild Rose   *Rosa sayi*

Raspberry and Thimbleberry *Rubus*

Known for edible, tasty berries, these shrubs are often armed with prickles. They grow up to 5 feet tall and have simple or, more frequently, compound leaves. Their white flowers have five separate petals and numerous stamens. Six *Rubus* species grow in Wyoming.

Raspberry and thimbleberry bloom in June and July and occur in partly moist to dry soils, often along roadsides and in other disturbed areas.

Wild red raspberry (*Rubus idaeus*) is a short-lived perennial with erect, prickly stems and branches. Its leaves are pinnately compound with three to five pointed leaflets. The small flowers have five reflexed sepals, five white petals, and numerous stamens. The flowers grow in open clusters along the branches. The red fruits are easy to spot and delicious to eat. Wild red raspberry occurs in disturbed or rocky soils along roadsides and streams in the foothills, montane, subalpine, and alpine zones and is widespread across western North America.

Thimbleberry (*Rubus parviflorus*) has smooth, woody stems and large, simple leaves, up to 7 inches across, with palmate lobes. Its showy white flowers grow up to 2 inches across. The tasty red berries, $\frac{1}{2}$ to $\frac{3}{4}$ inch broad, look like a thimble-shaped red raspberry with hair on their surface. The dried sepals show prominently behind the ripe berry. It grows in moist places, often along streams, in the foothills and montane zones from southern British Columbia and Alberta to New Mexico.

Creeping Sibbaldia *Sibbaldia procumbens*

Creeping Sibbaldia is a low-growing plant that has small flowers with five small, greenish yellow petals surrounded by five large, greenish yellow sepals. There are five green, leafy bracts that surround the entire flower. The palmately compound leaves, with three oval, toothed leaflets, resemble the leaves of wild strawberry. Unlike strawberry, these toothed leaflets have flat tips and are notched. This is the only *Sibbaldia* species in Wyoming.

Carolus Linnaeus named this plant in honor of Sir Robert Sibbald, a physician and teacher in Edinburgh, Scotland. Creeping Sibbaldia is very common; it blooms from June to early August and grows in moist soils in the subalpine and alpine zones. It is widespread in western North America.

Wild Red Raspberry flowers and fruit
Rubus idaeus

Thimbleberry
Rubus parviflorus

Creeping Sibbaldia
Sibbaldia procumbens

Western Mountain Ash   *Sorbus scopulina*

These shrubs or small trees grow in erect clumps that are 3 to 12 feet tall. The leaves are pinnately compound and have eleven to thirteen leaflets with pointed tips. Flat-topped clusters of seventy to two hundred small white flowers bloom in June and are followed by colorful bunches of bright orange berries in late summer and fall. Although the berries are bitter, they are not poisonous and provide fall and winter food for birds. Mountain ash is often planted as an ornamental tree. Two *Sorbus* species occur in Wyoming.

Western mountain ash grows in moist, shaded thickets along streams in the foothills and montane zones from the Yukon to New Mexico.

Spirea   *Spirea*

These woody shrubs have pretty, showy flowers and grow 1 to 4 feet tall. They have simple, oval leaves with rounded teeth. The small flowers have five petals and a center of yellow stamens; they grow in slightly rounded clusters along, and on the ends of, the branches.

Two *Spirea* species occur in Wyoming: meadowsweet and subalpine spirea. They inhabit streambanks and moist slopes.

Meadowsweet (*Spirea betulifolia*) grows up to 4 feet tall and has alternate leaves that have lobes and rounded teeth. Flowers have five white petals, many yellow stamens, and grow in flat-topped clusters. Native Americans used meadowsweet to treat a variety of illnesses; it is well known as a pain reliever and is related to aspirin. It grows in moist sites in the foothills and montane zones. Meadowsweet blooms in June and July and occurs from southern British Columbia, Alberta, and Saskatchewan to South Dakota, Wyoming, Montana, and Oregon.

Subalpine spirea (*Spirea splendens*), with stems that are usually less than 15 inches tall, is topped with clusters of small, rosy pink flowers with protruding stamens. Found in moist stream drainages in the subalpine zone, it occurs in Yellowstone and Grand Teton National Parks north in the Rocky Mountains to southern British Columbia and Alberta.

Western Mountain Ash flowers and fruit
Sorbus scopulina

Meadowsweet
Spirea betulifolia

Subalpine Spirea
Spirea splendens

ST. JOHN'S WORT FAMILY   Hypericaceae

The species of this family are characterized by leaves covered with small black dots. The flowers have five petals and numerous bunches of protruding stamens. This small family has three genera with three hundred species that occur in temperate regions worldwide.

St. John's Wort   *Hypericum formosum*

This spreading, perennial plant has many stems that are 4 to 24 inches tall and slightly fleshy, oval, opposite leaves. Its yellow flowers, up to $^3/_4$ inch across, have five triangular sepals and five oval petals with a distinct point. There may be as many as one hundred yellow stamens protruding beyond the petals. Small black dots cover the margins of the leaves, petals, and sepals. St. John's wort, long used as an herbal remedy, has antiviral properties. There are only two *Hypericum* species in Wyoming. Klamath weed *(Hypericum perforatum)* is a troublesome weed that was introduced from Europe and is now widespread in the western United States. It has long linear sepals and grows in disturbed sites.

St. John's wort blooms in July and August and grows in moist soils in the foothills, montane, subalpine, and alpine zones from southern British Columbia and Alberta to New Mexico.

SANDALWOOD FAMILY   Santalaceae

The sandalwood family is found nearly worldwide, mostly in warm, arid regions. These plants have green foliage and are partial parasites that grow on the roots of other plants. Flowers are small with five petal-like sepals united at the base and five stamens.

Bastard Toadflax   *Comandra umbellata*

Bastard toadflax grows on the roots of other plants to obtain part of its nutrients. It is not a large plant, up to 12 inches tall, and it commonly grows with sagebrush. The simple, alternate leaves, up to $1^1/_2$ inches long, are bluish green, fleshy, smooth, and narrowly elliptical. Its small, whitish or cream-colored flowers are arranged in a rounded cluster at the tops of the stems. Bastard toadflax has no petals, only five waxy, pointed, petal-like sepals. This is the only *Comandra* species in Wyoming.

Bastard toadflax blooms from May to August, grows in dry and sandy soils in the plains, steppe, and foothills zones, and is widespread in western North America.

St. John's Wort
Hypericum formosum

Bastard Toadflax
Comandra umbellata

SAXIFRAGE FAMILY   Saxifragaceae

The herbs in the saxifrage family have mostly basal leaves and flowers with five sepals and five petals that occur in a cluster along or on top of a naked stem. There are 650 species, which are most common and numerous in cold, northern temperate and arctic regions worldwide.

Common Alumroot   *Heuchera parvifolia*
Common alumroot has basal leaves with flowers along the top of a naked stem that grows 8 to 24 inches tall. The round, leathery leaves have rounded teeth and are covered with sticky glandular hair. The flowers are small and have five greenish yellow petals. Alumroot is used as an herbal medicine and is not poisonous but may be quite sour. Four *Heuchera* species grow in Wyoming.

Common alumroot blooms from May to July. It favors rocky slopes, grows in rock fissures in all vegetation zones, and is widespread in the western United States.

Woodland Star   *Lithophragma parviflorum*
Woodland star has a few basal leaves and a few smaller leaves along the slender stems that grow 4 to 12 inches tall. Its leaves are palmately divided into narrow segments. Three to eleven pretty, delicate flowers occur on each stem and have five white petals deeply divided into three to five narrow, pointed lobes. Three *Lithophragma* species occur in Wyoming. They bloom early in the season in May and June.

Also called *starflower* because its flowers resemble stars, woodland star grows in moist, rich soil in meadows and aspen groves in the foothills and montane zones from southern British columbia and Montana to South Dakota, Colorado, and Utah.

Mitrewort   *Mitella pentandra*
Living along mountain streams, mitrewort has heart-shaped basal leaves with prominent veins and toothed, shallow lobes. The tiny, greenish yellow flowers grow along the upper half of a leafless stalk. The flowers have five sepals turned back at the tip, five petals that are divided into five to eleven threadlike segments, and five stamens. It is also called *bishop's cap,* apparently because the seeds that have two beaks resemble a bishop's miter, which has two points. Two *Mitella* species grow in Wyoming.

Mitrewort blooms in June and July and grows in shady forests in the montane, subalpine, and alpine zones. It is widespread in western North America.

Common Alumroot
Heuchera parvifolia

Woodland Star
Lithophragma parviflorum

Mitrewort   *Mitella pentandra*

Grass of Parnassus   *Parnassia fimbriata*

Grass of Parnassus has round, glossy green, basal leaves and a single, heart-shaped leaf growing on the upper half of the stem. Its solitary white flowers, on stems 4 to 8 inches tall, have five petals that are fringed with hair near their base. This wildflower can often be seen blooming alongside brook saxifrage (*Saxifraga odontoloma*). Four *Parnassia* species grow in Wyoming.

Some botanists place grass of Parnassus in the grass of Parnassus family (Parnassiaceae). It blooms mid-July and grows in wet meadows along streams in the montane, subalpine, and alpine zones. It is widespread in the western United States.

Saxifrage   *Saxifraga*

Saxifrages typically have basal leaves and tall, leafless, unbranched stems. Their small flowers have five separate, white to greenish white petals; the flowers occur in dense to open branched clusters. Saxifrages bloom early in the season—May in lower elevations to July and August in the alpine zone.

There are thirteen different species of saxifrage in Wyoming, mostly seen in higher elevations of the mountains growing in moist soils and along streams in the foothills, montane, subalpine, and alpine zones.

Brook saxifrage (*Saxifraga odontoloma*) has shiny, green leaves that are round in outline and have scalloped margins. The small flowers have white petals with a purplish tinge and red-tipped stamens. It grows along the edges of shady streams and springs in the montane zone and is widespread in western North America.

Snowball saxifrage (*Saxifraga rhomboidea*) has diamond-shaped leaves with a single, dense, round flower cluster on the tip of a leafless stalk that grows up to 8 inches tall. It grows in moist areas, often near melting snowbanks, in the foothills, montane, subalpine, and alpine zones from Montana to New Mexico.

Oregon saxifrage (*Saxifraga subapetala*) has lance-shaped basal leaves that are not glossy. Flowers occur in small, rounded clusters at intervals along a tall, branched stem, which grows up to 24 inches tall. Found on moist, rocky soils in the montane, subalpine, and alpine zones, it occurs from Montana to Colorado west to Nevada and Idaho.

Grass of Parnassus
Parnassia fimbriata

Brook Saxifrage
Saxifraga odontoloma

Oregon Saxifrage
Saxifraga subapetala

Snowball Saxifrage
Saxifraga rhomboidea

Telesonix　*Telesonix heucheriformis*

This uncommon wildflower, found growing mostly on limestone or dolomite cliffs, has basal leaves that are covered with sticky glandular hair. The leaves, round in outline, are scalloped with rounded teeth. Flowers are composed of five small, reddish purple petals that are enclosed by five large, brick red sepals; the flowers occur in a bell-shaped arrangement and are clustered on erect stems that grow 3 to 8 inches tall. Two *Telesonix* species occur in Wyoming. They bloom in June and July.

Telesonix can be found in the montane, subalpine, and alpine zones from southern Alberta to western South Dakota, Wyoming, Idaho, and Utah.

STICKLEAF FAMILY　　　　　　　　　　Loasaceae

The stickleaf family is composed of coarse herbs that are covered with barbed hair and sport showy flowers, which open at night. The flowers are conspicuous with five sepals, five petals (some flowers may have eight or ten), and many spreading stamens. Most of the 250 species occur in North and South America in warm climates.

Blazing Star　*Mentzelia*

These robust plants are covered with barbed hair and have large flowers that open at dusk and close in the morning sun. The flowers occur in branched clusters along the upper portion of the stem and seem to glow in moonlight; the radiating stamens cause them to look like stars. These two features give rise to the plants' common names. They have rough, alternate leaves that are pinnately divided into pointed lobes. There are thirteen *Mentzelia* species in Wyoming.

Blazing stars usually bloom during July and August and grow on barren hills and sandy or gravelly roadsides in the plains, steppe, and montane zones.

Giant evening star *(Mentzelia decapetala)* grows 12 to 36 inches tall and has large, cream-colored or off-white flowers that are 2 to 3 inches across. Each flower has ten petals and numerous long stamens that fan out in all directions. It occurs in plains, steppe, foothills, and montane zones mostly east of the Rocky Mountains from Alberta to Mexico.

Smooth-stem blazing star *(Mentzelia laevicaulis)* has large yellow flowers, up to 3 inches across, with five pointed petals. Stems grow up to 18 inches tall. It is found in the steppe, foothills, and montane zones in British Columbia, Montana, and Wyoming.

Telesonix *Telesonix heucheriformis*

Giant Evening Star
Mentzelia decapetala

Smooth-Stem Blazing Star
Mentzelia laevicaulis

STONECROP FAMILY   Crassulaceae

Species of the stonecrop family are characterized by succulent, simple leaves and star-shaped flowers. Flowers have five sharply pointed petals and ten stamens and grow in terminal clusters. Many species are grown as ornamentals in rock gardens. They occur mostly in dry regions worldwide.

Stonecrop *Sedum*

Stonecrop plants have fleshy leaves and relatively short stems that grow 2 to 8 inches tall. The succulent leaves are alternate and usually crowded on the stem. The flowers have five separate, elliptical or lance-shaped, pointed petals. All parts of these plants are edible and make tasty trail snacks. Six *Sedum* species occur in Wyoming.

Stonecrops occur in various habitats in all vegetation zones.

King's crown *(Sedum integrifolium)* has flattened, oval leaves, up to ¹/₂ inch long, and dark red to purple flowers in dense, flat-topped clusters at the ends of the stems. It grows up to 6 inches tall and blooms mid-July to August. It is found in rocky, open, moist soils and rocky cliffs in the subalpine and alpine zones throughout western North America.

Lanceleaf stonecrop *(Sedum lanceolatum)* has alternate leaves that often drop off early; stems and leaves are often reddish. It has bright yellow flowers that look like a star when viewed from above. The flowers are up to ¹/₂ inch across and occur in dense, flat-topped clusters at the tops of stems that grow up to 8 inches tall. The stamens are yellow and extend beyond the petals. Lanceleaf stonecrop blooms from June to mid-August. It grows in dry soils, often on roadcuts, in all vegetation zones and is common in western North America.

Rose crown *(Sedum rhodanthum)* has oblong leaves and pale pink to dark pink flowers clustered on the tips of leafy stems that grow up to 12 inches tall. It flowers in July and August and grows in wet meadows and near streams in the montane, subalpine, and alpine zones from Montana to New Mexico.

King's Crown   *Sedum integrifolium*

Lanceleaf Stonecrop
Sedum lanceolatum

Rose Crown
Sedum rhodanthum

SUMAC FAMILY   Anacardiaceae

Mostly tropical in distribution, members of this family are woody plants, some with allergenic properties. A few species are found in temperate regions of North America. They have compound leaves and flowers with five united sepals, five separate petals, and five stamens.

Skunkbush Sumac *Rhus aromatica*

Skunkbush sumac is a rounded, woody shrub that grows up to 6 feet tall. The compound leaves have leaflets with three, scalloped lobes. Its tiny, light-yellowish green flowers grow in compact, knobby clusters on the stems. They appear before the leaves emerge in the spring. The plant has a strong, resinous odor, but it does not smell like a skunk as its common name suggests. The reddish orange berries, up to ½ inch broad, have hairy, sticky skin. Native Americans and pioneers used them to make a tart beverage similar to lemonade. Two *Rhus* species occur in Wyoming.

Skunkbush sumac grows on dry, rocky hillsides and along streams and roadcuts in the plains, steppe, and foothills. It is widespread in western North America.

Poison Ivy *Toxicodendron rydbergii*

This leafy perennial has partly woody stems and grows 4 to 30 inches tall in large patches. Oils in the leaves, stems, and berries may cause skin blisters within a few days of contact. Use caution around this plant since it can cause a serious allergic reaction in some people. Learn to recognize the bright green, palmately compound leaves that have three oval, pointed leaflets. These leaves turn gold, bright reddish orange, or scarlet in the fall. Small white flowers, which hide beneath the leaves, appear in May and June. The greenish white berries occur in small clusters and may persist on the stems through the winter. This is the only *Toxicodendron* species in Wyoming.

Poison ivy grows in sunny, well-drained, moist areas along streams, riverbanks, and rock edges in the plains and foothills throughout western North America.

Skunkbush Sumac fruit   *Rhus aromatica*
Inset: Skunkbush Sumac flowers

Poison Ivy   *Toxicodendron rydbergii*

Poison Ivy flowers

SUNFLOWER FAMILY   Asteraceae

This very large family of herbs and shrubs has nearly twenty thousand species that are found in dry, temperate climates worldwide. The plants are characterized by flower heads that look like a single flower but are actually composed of many small flowers in a dense cluster on top of a broad stem. There are two types of flowers: tube-shaped disk flowers that have no petals, and ray flowers that have a strap-shaped petal. The disk flowers occur in the center of the flower head and the ray flowers are positioned on the outer edge. Flower heads of sunflower species can have all ray flowers, all disk flowers, or both ray and disk flowers. There are 109 genera and 450 species in Wyoming. Because of the large number of species, we have only described the most common and showy genera.

Yarrow *Achillea millefolium*

Yarrow has a strong, aromatic odor and finely divided, feathery leaves; it grows up to 18 inches tall in clumps. The flower heads, ¼ inch across, have three to five white, ray flowers and a center of light-yellow disk flowers. They are grouped in flat-topped clusters. Leaves and stems are sticky to the touch. Yarrow has been used for centuries as an herbal medicine to treat burns, stop bleeding, and treat colds. This is the only *Achillea* species in Wyoming.

Yarrow blooms from June to September and grows in dry to moist soils, often along roads and in disturbed sites, in all vegetation zones. It is widespread in western North America.

Mountain Dandelion *Agoseris*

These wildflowers have leafless flower stems that are 6 to 12 inches tall and narrow, lance-shaped basal leaves. The leaf margins are entire or may have a few lobes or scattered teeth. When cut, the stems and leaves ooze milky juice. The solitary flower heads have only ray flowers and look shaggy because the rays are not all the same length. Three *Agoseris* species occur in Wyoming.

You can find mountain dandelions blooming in May in the plains and steppe and as late as August in the subalpine and alpine zones. They grow in dry to moist, sunny meadows in all vegetation zones.

Orange mountain dandelion (*Agoseris aurantiaca*) has orange ray flowers that turn pink or purple with age. It grows in dry meadows and forest openings in the montane, subalpine, and alpine zones from southern British Columbia and Alberta to New Mexico.

Pale mountain dandelion (*Agoseris glauca*) has yellow flower heads on slender stalks and commonly occurs in all vegetation zones throughout the western United States. Sometimes called *false dandelion,* pale mountain dandelion bears a strong resemblance to the common dandelion (*Taraxacum officinale*), an introduced plant

Top: Yarrow
Achillea millefolium

Bottom left: Orange
Mountain Dandelion
Agoseris aurantiaca

Bottom right:
Pale Mountain Dandelion
Agoseris glauca

from Europe. Pale mountain dandelion flower heads have fewer ray flowers and the leaves are narrower and less numerous than the common dandelion.

Pearly Everlasting   *Anaphalis margaritacea*

Pearly everlasting, often seen along forest roads, spreads in patches and grows 12 to 18 inches tall. The opposite, grayish green stem leaves are narrow with entire margins and are covered underneath with white, woolly hair. Its small flower heads, up to ⅓ inch across, are composed of yellow disk flowers surrounded by pearly white bracts; they grow in dense, flat-topped clusters on the stems. The flowers are papery when dry and persist until winter. Pearly everlasting blooms from July to September. It resembles pussytoes (*Antennaria* species), which do not have tall, leafy stems and generally bloom in May and June. This is the only *Anaphalis* species in Wyoming.

Pearly everlasting grows in full sun in the foothills and montane zones and is common throughout western North America.

Pussytoes   *Antennaria*

Pussytoes have creeping stems that form spreading mats of basal leaves. Leaves are simple and covered with hair, giving them a whitish gray color. Small, rounded flower heads, up to ¼ inch across, are comprised of disk flowers and are usually grouped in clusters. There are more than eighteen *Antennaria* species in Wyoming.

Pussytoes bloom in April and May at low elevations and as late as July at high elevations. They can be found in dry, sunny sites in all vegetation zones and are widespread in western North America.

Tall pussytoes (*Antennaria anaphaloides*) has elliptical leaves that grow up to 8 inches long; most of them are basal, but a few small leaves occur on the stem. The stem grows 4 to 10 inches tall and is crowned with up to fifty white flower heads in flat-topped clusters. It is common in open, dry woods and sagebrush flats in the steppe, foothills, montane, subalpine, and alpine zones from southern British Columbia and Alberta to Idaho and Colorado.

Alpine pussytoes (*Antennaria media*) forms large mats of gray, egg-shaped leaves that are about 1 inch long. It has white flower heads with brownish outer bracts that occur on flower stalks that grow up to 4 inches tall. Three to seven flower heads occur in terminal clusters. It grows in gravelly soils in the montane, subalpine, and alpine zones from southern British Columbia and Alberta to Colorado and Utah.

Rosy pussytoes (*Antennaria microphylla*) has up to nine light- to dark-pink flower heads in clusters. It grows as a dense mat of small, gray, oval leaves with several flower clusters on stalks that are 3 to 12 inches long. It occurs in rocky areas in the plains, steppe, and foothills and is widespread in western North America.

Pearly Everlasting
Anaphalis margaritacea

Tall Pussytoes
Antennaria anaphaloides

Alpine Pussytoes
Antennaria media

Rosy Pussytoes
Antennaria microphylla

Arnica *Arnica*

These perennial wildflowers have large, yellow flower heads and are readily identified by their stems and leaves that are covered with glandular hair, which makes the foliage feel sticky and rough. The simple, opposite leaves are elliptical to heart shaped with entire margins. Flower heads have nine to twenty ray flowers that are sometimes notched at the tip and yellow disk flowers. Arnicas grow from 8 to 24 inches tall, often in large patches, producing colorful displays in mountain meadows and open coniferous forests. Oils produced in the foliage are sometimes extracted for herbal use. Thirteen species of arnica occur in Wyoming.

Arnicas can be found in full sun to partial shade in the steppe, foothills, montane, subalpine, and alpine zones.

Heartleaf arnica *(Arnica cordifolia)* has solitary flower heads and two to four heart-shaped leaves that grow up to 4 inches long and almost as broad. It has basal leaves and a smaller pair of oval leaves halfway up the stem. Heartleaf arnica blooms from May to August. It occurs in the montane and subalpine zones and is commonly seen in dry, lodgepole pine forests. It is widespread in western North America.

Hairy arnica *(Arnica mollis)* has three or four pairs of stiff, elliptical leaves, up to 2 inches long, and one or more flower heads per stem. It blooms in July and August and is common in montane and subalpine meadows. It occurs in the Rocky Mountains of Canada south to New Mexico and Utah.

Rayless arnica *(Arnica parryi)* is noteworthy because it is the only species of arnica that lacks ray flowers and has only disk flowers. Several flower heads occur singly or clustered on branch tips. Rayless arnica is also known as *Parry's arnica*. It blooms from June to August and grows in the foothills, montane, and subalpine zones from southern Alberta and British Columbia to Colorado and Utah.

Top left: Heartleaf Arnica
Arnica cordifolia

Top right: Rayless Arnica
Arnica parryi

Bottom: Hairy Arnica
Arnica mollis

Sagebrush *Artemisia*

Twenty-one species of this large genus occur in Wyoming. They range from large, woody shrubs growing across the steppe to diminutive plants in the alpine zone. These plants are strongly aromatic and have flower heads composed of disk flowers. Leaves are alternate and may be entire or divided. These wildflowers bloom from July to September.

Various sagebrush species are found in all vegetation zones.

Prairie sagewort *(Artemisia frigida)* has mat-forming, woody stems that grow 4 to 16 inches tall. It has finely divided, grayish green leaves that are densely covered with hair. Hairy, yellowish flower heads occur in erect clusters. It grows in dry soils in the plains, steppe, foothills, and montane zones and is common and widespread from the Great Plains to eastern California and Oregon.

Alpine sagewort *(Artemisia scopulorum)* is a high mountain plant that has finely divided, hairy leaves. It has greenish yellow flower heads in erect clusters along an erect stem that grows up to 12 inches tall. They drop copious amounts of pollen when in full bloom. Alpine sagewort grows in the alpine zone and occurs from southwestern Montana to New Mexico and Utah.

Wyoming big sagebrush *(Artemisia tridentata)* is the grayish shrub seen over large areas of Wyoming. In some places it grows more than 6 feet tall. The wedge-shaped leaves have three rounded lobes at their tip and are hairy and strongly aromatic. It has grayish green flowers heads clustered along upright stems and held above the leafy branches. The grayish bark shreds off older bushes in strips. Wyoming big sagebrush blooms late in the summer and is widespread on dry plains and slopes in the steppe, foothills, montane, and subalpine zones from southern British Columbia and Alberta to New Mexico and California.

Prairie Sagewort
Artemisia frigida

Alpine Sagewort
Artemisia scopulorum

Wyoming Big Sagebrush
Artemisia tridentata

Ragleaf Bahia *Bahia dissecta*

Ragleaf bahia, easily recognized by its open-branched stems that grow 8 to 32 inches tall, has pinnately compound leaves with narrow leaflets; each leaflet has three lobes on its tip. The glandular foliage is sticky. The dainty flower heads, up to 1 inch across, have ten to fifteen yellow ray flowers with blunt tips and three shallow teeth. This is the only *Bahia* species in Wyoming.

Ragleaf bahia occurs in gravelly, sandy soil in open sites, often in pinyon-juniper woodland, in the foothills and montane zones. It blooms in August and September; look for it from southeastern Wyoming to Colorado, New Mexico, and Arizona.

Balsamroot *Balsamorhiza*

The golden yellow blooms of balsamroots blanket hillsides in late May and early June, signaling a return to warm weather. They are herbaceous perennials with large, grayish green basal leaves. They grow 8 to 28 inches tall. Leaves are hairy and, depending on the species, vary from entire to notched margins. Large, solitary flower heads, 2 to 4 inches across, have twelve to twenty-two yellow ray flowers and centers of yellow or gold disk flowers. Native Americans roasted the edible roots and ate the leaves as greens. Four *Balsamorhiza* species grow in Wyoming.

Balsamroots grow in dry, stony soils on hillsides and meadows in the steppe, foothills, and montane zones.

Hoary balsamroot *(Balsamorhiza incana)* has densely hairy, deeply notched basal leaves that grow up to 8 inches long. It blooms in May and June and is found only in Idaho, Montana, and Wyoming.

Arrowleaf balsamroot *(Balsamorhiza sagittata)*, often associated with Wyoming big sagebrush *(Artemisia tridentata),* has entire, distinctive, arrowhead-shaped leaves that grow up to 10 inches long. It occurs from southern British Columbia and Alberta to Colorado, and west to California.

Ragleaf Bahia
Bahia dissecta

Hoary Balsamroot
Balsamorhiza incana

Arrowleaf Balsamroot   *Balsamorhiza sagittata*

Tasselflower   *Brickellia grandiflora*

Tasselflower has leafy stems that grow 8 to 32 inches tall. The triangular, toothed leaves usually dry up and fall off the lower stem by flowering time. The tassel-like flower heads of cream-colored disk flowers bloom in July and August and grow in drooping, open clusters at the tops of the stems. Three *Brickellia* species grow in Wyoming.

Tasselflower grows in dry, rocky sites in the foothills and montane zones from Washington and Montana to California, Arizona, and New Mexico.

Douglas' Dusty Maiden   *Chaenactis douglasii*

Named for David Douglas, a naturalist in western North America in the early 1800s, Douglas' dusty maiden has pinnately divided leaves that grow up to $4\frac{1}{2}$ inches long. The coarse, hairy leaves are whitish to grayish green and have curling segments. Because of these curling segments, the leaves never appear flat. Its whitish to cream-colored flower heads have no ray flowers, only fifty to seventy disk flowers that occur on stems, which grow up to 20 inches tall.

Douglas' dusty maiden blooms from May to July and grows in sandy or gravelly soils in all vegetation zones; it is widespread in the western United States.

Thistle   *Cirsium*

Thistles have spiny, branched stems and spiny leaves that are toothed to pinnately divided. The globe-shaped flower heads have spiny bracts and are comprised of only disk flowers. The leaves, stems, and roots of some thistles are edible when peeled and cooked, while others are bitter. There are eighteen species of thistle in Wyoming, some native and some introduced from Europe and Asia.

Thistles grow on dry to moist, often disturbed sites in all vegetation zones.

Prairie thistle (*Cirsium canescens*) grows up to 40 inches tall and has hairy, cobweblike leaves, 6 to 12 inches long, with wavy, deeply cut margins. One to two globe-shaped, dull white flower heads occur per stem; they are up to $3/4$ inch broad and surrounded by spiny bracts. Blooming in late May and June, it grows in the plains, steppe, and foothills east of the Continental Divide from Montana to Colorado.

Elk thistle (*Cirsium scariosum*) is a leafy plant that grows up to 40 inches tall. Round, white to lavender flower heads occur in dense clusters and are hidden among the crowded, upper leaves. Elk thistle blooms from June to August and grows in moist meadows in the foothills, montane, and subalpine zones from southern British Columbia and Alberta to New Mexico and Arizona.

Tasselflower
Brickellia grandiflora

Douglas' Dusty Maiden
Chaenactis douglasii

'rairie Thistle   *Cirsium canescens*

Elk Thistle   *Cirsium scariosum*

Common Tickseed *Coreopsis tinctoria*
Common tickseed is a plant of the Great Plains. It has slender, branched stems that grow 20 inches tall. Its leaves are opposite and once or twice pinnately divided into thin, narrow segments. The showy flower heads grow on the ends of slender branches and have yellow ray flowers with a maroon band near their base and reddish brown disk flowers. They bloom in August and September, are easily cultivated, and are found in many flower gardens and wildflower seed mixtures. Two *Coreopsis* species grow in Wyoming.

Common tickseed grows in places where there is some moisture, such as roadside ditches and grassy marshes, often in sandy soil in the plains zone. It is widespread in the Great Plains.

Limestone Hawksbeard *Crepis intermedia*
Limestone hawksbeard has basal leaves with a few leaves on the stems. Five to ten flower heads grow on each branched stem, which grow up to 6 inches tall and ooze milky juice when cut. The distinctive leaves are deeply divided into wavy-edged, sharp-toothed lobes that point backwards. Nine *Crepis* species occur in Wyoming.

Limestone hawksbeard blooms from May to July and grows in dry, open sites, often in limestone-rich soils, in the steppe, foothills, and montane zones; it is widespread in western North America.

Purple Coneflower *Echinacea angustifolia*
This plant grows 24 to 36 inches tall and has erect, leafy, coarse stems that are covered with stiff hair. The leaves grow up to 8 inches long and 6 inches wide and are dark green, stiff, leathery, and lance shaped. Showy, reddish purple flower heads have drooping ray flowers that are cleft at the tip. The central cone is covered with dark purple disk flowers. Echinacea, one of the most popular herbal medicines on the market today, is derived from purple coneflower. This is the only *Echinacea* species in Wyoming.

Purple coneflower blooms in July and August and grows in open, rocky prairies along dry roadsides in the plains. It occurs in the Great Plains from Saskatchewan to Texas.

Common Tickseed
Coreopsis tinctoria

Purple Coneflower
Echinacea angustifolia

Limestone Hawksbeard *Crepis intermedia*

Common Rabbitbrush *Ericameria nauseosa*

Golden blossoms of common rabbitbrush brighten the steppe in August and September. This densely branched shrub grows 8 to 24 inches tall and has a compact, rounded shape. The leaves are narrow, short, and grayish green. The bright yellow flower heads, ¼ inch across, lack ray flowers and grow in open to dense clusters of several flower heads at the branch tips. It is sometimes called *rubber rabbitbrush* because its stems contain latex. Three *Ericameria* species occur in Wyoming.

Formerly known as *Chrysothamnus nauseosus,* common rabbitbrush grows on dry soils, often along roadsides in the plains, steppe, foothills, and montane zones from southern British Columbia, Alberta, and Saskatchewan south across the western United States.

Daisy *Erigeron*

These wildflowers range from small alpine forms to more robust plants in lower elevations. Their leaves are often simple and mostly basal with some smaller stem leaves. Flower heads usually have more than twenty-five ray flowers and may be white, pink, blue, or purple. There are forty-four *Erigeron* species in Wyoming, many of which closely resemble, and are difficult to distinguish from, other species in the sunflower family.

Daisies are found in sunny meadows, slopes, and woods in all vegetation zones from the plains to the alpine zone. They are common and widespread in western North America.

Cutleaf daisy *(Erigeron compositus)* can be identified by its leaves, which are divided into three parts, and flower heads that have twenty to sixty narrow, white ray flowers and a center of gold disk flowers. Some plants, called *gold buttons,* lack ray flowers altogether. Cutleaf daisy blooms in May and June and grows from 1½ to 10 inches tall. It is abundant in heavily grazed areas, and land managers use it as an indicator of overgrazing. It is found in the foothills, montane, subalpine, and alpine zones throughout western North America.

Common Rabbitbrush *Ericameria nauseosa*

Cutleaf Daisy
Erigeron compositus

Gold Buttons
Erigeron compositus

Bear River fleabane daisy (*Erigeron ursinus*) has entire, elliptical leaves and grows up to 10 inches tall. Flower heads are solitary with thirty to one hundred ray flowers. They are blue to pinkish purple with yellow disk flowers and are up to 1½ inches across. Bear River fleabane daisy blooms in June and early July and grows in moist meadows and grassy slopes of the montane, subalpine, and alpine zones. It is common in the mountains and occurs from Montana and Idaho to Colorado and Utah.

Engelmann's Aster   *Eucephalus engelmannii*

Engelmann's aster grows up to 18 inches tall and has alternate, lance-shaped to elliptical leaves that are 2 to 4 inches long. White ray flowers are attached irregularly around the yellow disk flowers, giving the plant a ragged appearance. Single flower heads grow on branches at the tips of stems. Named for George Engelmann, a German physician and botanist who collected plants in the Rocky Mountains in the mid-1800s, it was formerly called *Aster engelmannii*. Three *Eucephalus* species occur in Wyoming.

Engelmann's aster blooms from June to August and grows in shady aspen groves and conifer openings in the montane and subalpine zones; it occurs from southwestern Montana to Colorado and west to Utah.

Blanketflower   *Gaillardia aristata*

This wildflower grows 8 to 28 inches tall, has a solitary flower head, and hairy, rough stems and leaves. The lance-shaped basal leaves have entire margins. The stem leaves are either toothed or lobed. Blanketflower has sunflower-like heads that are large, showy, and up to 3 inches across. The yellow (sometimes orange or red) ray flowers are deeply notched into three lobes and surround a domed, orangish brown center of disk flowers. Blanketflower is often planted along highways and is common as a cultivated garden perennial. This is the only *Gaillardia* species in Wyoming.

Blanketflower blooms from June to September and grows in dry soil in the plains, steppe, foothills, and montane zones from southern British Columbia, Alberta, and Saskatchewan to Arizona and New Mexico.

Bear River Fleabane Daisy
Erigeron ursinus

Blanketflower
Gaillardia aristata

Engelmann's Aster *Eucephalus engelmannii*

Curlycup Gumweed   *Grindelia squarrosa*

This common, weedy plant has sticky, glandular foliage and an unpleasant odor. It grows 8 to 24 inches tall and has toothed, oblong leaves. Flower heads are 1 inch across and have yellow disk flowers and twenty-five to forty bright yellow ray flowers. Shiny, sticky, resinous bracts surround the flower head, are reflexed, and project outwards. Native Americans used curlycup gumweed as an herbal medicine and as chewing gum. Two *Grindelia* species occur in Wyoming.

Curlycup gumweed blooms from July to September and grows in dry, open, disturbed sites, often along roadsides, in the plains, steppe, foothills, and montane zones; it is common in the western United States.

Broom Snakeweed   *Gutierrezia sarothrae*

Broom snakeweed is a small shrub with slender, brittle, branched stems that grows 8 to 24 inches tall. The leaves are simple, narrow, and bright green. Flower heads, ¼ inch across, are composed of just a few yellow ray flowers; there are no disk flowers. Numerous flower heads occur in flat-topped clusters on the tops of the branches. Broom snakeweed blooms in August and September in areas that have been heavily grazed. This is the only *Gutierrezia* species in Wyoming.

Broom snakeweed grows in dry, sunny areas of the plains, steppe, and foothills throughout the western United States.

Nodding Little Sunflower   *Helianthella quinquenervis*

This robust plant grows 24 to 60 inches tall and has showy flower heads. The broad, elliptical basal leaves grow 4 to 9 inches long, are shiny, and have two prominent pairs of veins. A few pairs of opposite leaves also grow on the flower stem. The flower heads, comprised of lemon yellow ray flowers and golden disk flowers, turn downward, nodding on the tops of tall stems. Their centers, where the disk flowers are attached, are flat. Nodding little sunflower blooms in July, often over large areas in the open forest. Two *Helianthella* species grow in Wyoming.

Nodding little sunflower is found in semi-dry to moist meadows, frequently with aspen, in the foothills, montane, and subalpine zones. It is common and occurs from southern Idaho, southern Montana, and northwestern South Dakota to Arizona and New Mexico.

Curlycup Gumweed
Grindelia squarrosa

Nodding Little Sunflower
Helianthella quinquenervis

Broom Snakeweed   *Gutierrezia sarothrae*

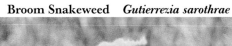

Sunflower *Helianthus*

Sunflowers provide bright color along roads and in weedy fields in late summer. They have coarse, rough foliage, opposite leaves on the lower stem, and alternate leaves on the upper stem. The golden yellow ray flowers surround centers of brown disk flowers. Seven species of sunflower grow in Wyoming.

Sunflowers grow in full sun in dry to moist, disturbed soils in the plains, steppe, and foothills.

Common sunflower *(Helianthus annuus)* is an annual that has heart-shaped leaves that are 4 to 8 inches long and several flower heads, 3 to 4 inches across, per stem. It grows up to 6 feet tall and is cultivated commercially for seeds and oil. This showy wildflower is the state flower of Kansas. Common sunflower blooms from July to September and grows in dry to slightly moist soils in disturbed sites. It is common and widespread in the western United States.

Nuttall's sunflower *(Helianthus nuttallii)* has lance-shaped leaves and many flower heads on well-branched stems that grow up to $3^{1}/_{2}$ feet tall. Flower heads may be up to $2^{1}/_{2}$ inches across. It blooms from July to September and grows in wet soils in meadows and streamsides from southern British Columbia, Alberta, and Saskatchewan to New Mexico and Arizona.

Dwarf sunflower *(Helianthus pumilis)* is a bushy, branched perennial with rough, hairy stems and leaves; it grows up to 15 inches tall. The leaves are stiff and lance shaped. Its flower heads may be 3 inches across and usually occur singly on branches with several flower heads per plant. Dwarf sunflower blooms in late June, July, and August. It grows in dry soils and along roadsides in the foothills and montane zones on the eastern flank of the Rocky Mountains from southern Montana to Colorado.

Top left: Common Sunflower
Helianthus annuus

Top right: Nuttall's Sunflower
Helianthus nuttallii

Bottom: Dwarf Sunflower
Helianthus pumilis

Golden Aster *Heterotheca villosa*

This golden, daisylike wildflower grows in clumps up to 12 inches tall. The elliptical leaves are very hairy, which gives them a grayish green color. Flower heads are 1 to 1$^1/_2$ inches across, have ten ray flowers with yellow disk flowers, and occur in short, few-flowered clusters; each cluster occurs on a separate stem. Four *Heterotheca* species grow in Wyoming.

Golden aster blooms from June to August and grows in sunny, often sandy soils, especially along roadsides, in the plains, steppe, foothills, and montane zones in the western United States.

White Hawkweed *Hieracium albiflorum*

White hawkweed has slender stems and basal leaves with white hair on their upper surface. White flower heads grow up to $^1/_2$ inch across and are composed of ray flowers only and blackish green bracts with sticky hair. The stems ooze milky juice when cut and grow 12 to 32 inches tall. Ten *Hieracium* species occur in Wyoming.

White hawkweed blooms from June to August and grows in moist, shaded forest openings in the foothills and montane zones; it is widespread in western North America.

Golden Aster *Heterotheca villosa*   White Hawkweed *Hieracium albiflorum*

Hymenoxys *Hymenoxys*

Hymenoxys species are perennial plants that can be identified by their drooping, yellow ray flowers that are notched at the tip into three distinct lobes. The flower heads have large, rounded centers of golden disk flowers. We described all three species that occur in Wyoming.

They grow in dry soils in all vegetation zones.

Old man of the mountain *(Hymenoxys grandiflora)* is a showy wildflower of high elevations that can grow 4 to 12 inches tall. The stems and pinnately divided basal leaves are woolly, hairy, and cobweblike at their base. Flower heads occur singly on each stem, have fifteen to thirty-five ray flowers, and grow up to 3 inches across. Sometimes called *rydbergia,* old man of the mountain blooms from late June to August and grows in open, gravelly slopes, often on limestone, in alpine areas from central Idaho, Montana, and Utah to Colorado.

Orange sneezeweed *(Hymenoxys hoopesii)* is a robust plant that grows 24 to 48 inches tall, has large, lance-shaped basal leaves that grow up to 12 inches long, and gold flower heads that are 2 to 3 inches across. The ray flowers droop slightly and are reflexed. Formerly called *Dugaldia hoopesii* or *Helenium hoopesii,* it grows in moist meadows, along streams and on open slopes, often in heavily grazed areas, in the foothills and montane zones. Orange sneezeweed blooms from June to August and occurs from southwestern Montana and central Idaho to Arizona and New Mexico.

Colorado rubber plant *(Hymenoxys richardsonii)* grows 12 to 24 inches tall and has pinnately compound leaves with narrow segments. The flower heads, up to 1 inch across, have drooping, yellow ray flowers. Flower heads occur singly on the ends of long, branched stems. This plant was at one time tested as a commercial source of rubber. Colorado rubber plant blooms in July and August and can be found in dry soils in the plains, steppe, foothills, montane, and subalpine zones from southern Alberta and Saskatchewan to Utah, Arizona, and Colorado.

Old Man of the Mountain
Hymenoxys grandiflora

Colorado Rubber Plant
Hymenoxys richardsonii

Orange Sneezeweed *Hymenoxys hoopesii*

Blue Lettuce *Lactuca oblongifolia*

This weedy plant has prickly, slender, nearly leafless stems that ooze milky juice when cut. It can grow up to 40 inches tall. The prickly lobes of its bluish green, lance-shaped leaves point backwards. Flower heads have twenty to fifty, bluish purple ray flowers. Blue lettuce is considered a noxious weed in some areas. Five *Lactuca* species occur in Wyoming.

Blue lettuce blooms from June to September and grows along roadsides, in disturbed sites, in pastures, and along streams in the plains, steppe, and foothills in the western United States.

Dotted Gayfeather *Liatris punctata*

This wildflower has slender, leafy flower stems that grow 4 to 24 inches tall. Entire, long, and narrow leaves are dotted with tiny pits. The flower heads, clustered along upright stems, have four to six pink or purple disk flowers but no ray flowers. Purple stamens protrude and impart a soft, feathery appearance to the flower heads. The plant has a starchy root that Native Americans used medicinally to treat kidney and liver problems, sore throats, and snakebites. Three *Liatris* species occur in Wyoming.

Dotted gayfeather blooms in August and September and grows in sandy soils in fields, along roadsides, and on rocky slopes in the plains and foothills and is widespread across the Great Plains.

Alpine Groundsel *Ligularia amplectens*

Alpine groundsel has solitary flower heads with eight to thirteen curled ray flowers and a cone-shaped center of gold disk flowers. The flower head grows up to 1½ inches across. The basal leaves are oblong and the stem leaves are narrow and elliptical with rough, toothed margins. Black-tipped bracts surround the ray flowers. It was formerly classified as *Senecio amplectens*. Two *Ligularia* species occur in Wyoming.

Alpine groundsel blooms in July and August and grows in rocky soils in the subalpine and alpine zones from southern Wyoming and central Utah to Colorado and New Mexico.

Top left: Blue Lettuce
Lactuca oblongifolia

Top right:
Dotted Gayfeather
Liatris punctata

Bottom:
Alpine Groundsel
Ligularia amplectens

Showy Skeletonweed   *Lygodesmia grandiflora*
Showy skeletonweed has several naked, jointed stems that grow 4 to 12 inches
tall and ooze milky juice when cut. The basal leaves are narrow and grasslike
with entire margins. Its pink flower heads, which occur singly on the stems
in July and August, have six to fifteen ray flowers that are notched at their tips
and no disk flowers. Also known as *milkpink,* its stems resemble chicory *(Chicorium
intybus),* an introduced weed. Chicory grows much taller than showy skeletonweed,
from 1 to 5 feet, has basal leaves with teeth, and sky blue flowers. Two *Lygodesmia*
species occur in Wyoming.

Showy skeletonweed grows in gravelly, sandy soils in the plains, steppe,
and foothills from central Wyoming to western Colorado, and west to Idaho,
Utah, and New Mexico.

Alpine Aster   *Oreostemma alpigenum*
This low-growing, early-blooming alpine aster has clusters of narrow, elliptical,
smooth basal leaves. The solitary flower heads, on stalks 4 to 8 inches tall, are
comprised of twenty purple ray flowers with centers of gold disk flowers. It
blooms in July and August. This wildflower was formerly called *Aster alpigenus*.
This is the only *Oreostemma* species in Wyoming.

Alpine aster grows in rocky soils in the subalpine and alpine zones. It is
found in western Montana and western Wyoming to Washington, and south
to the mountains of California and Nevada.

Wooly Groundsel   *Packera cana*
Wooly groundsel has densely hairy, elliptical basal leaves. The branched stems
grow 4 to 10 inches tall and have flat-topped clusters of six to fifteen flower
heads. The flower heads are about $1/2$ inch across and have six or seven yellow
ray flowers around a center of gold disk flowers. This plant was formerly called
Senecio canus. There are fifteen *Packera* species in Wyoming; they were formerly
considered part of the genus *Senecio*.

Wooly groundsel blooms in May and June and grows in dry, rocky sites in
all vegetation zones. It is very common and widespread in the northern Great
Plains and in the mountains of western North America.

Showy Skeletonweed
Lygodesmia grandiflora

Wooly Groundsel
Packera cana

Alpine Aster *Oreostemma alpigenum*

Golden Curlyhead   *Pyrrocoma crocea*

This wildflower has solitary, bright yellow or orange flower heads with thirty to ninety curling, drooping ray flowers and numerous gold disk flowers. The flower head, up to 3 inches across, occurs on stems that grow up to 12 inches tall. There are oblong basal leaves and smaller, smooth, shiny, elliptical stem leaves. Golden curlyhead was formerly named *Haplopappus croceus*. Six *Pyrrocoma* species occur in Wyoming.

Golden curlyhead grows in meadows and forest openings in the montane and subalpine zones. It is found only in the Medicine Bow Range in Wyoming south to New Mexico, Utah, and Arizona.

Upright Prairie Coneflower   *Ratibida columnifera*

This prairie wildflower has branched stems and grows 12 to 36 inches tall. Most of the basal leaves are divided into narrow, pointed segments. Flower heads are composed of three to seven yellow ray flowers around a raised cone of dark red, disk flowers. This showy wildflower is becoming more common as it spreads from highway plantings and flower gardens. Two *Ratibida* species grow in Wyoming.

Upright prairie coneflower blooms from June to September and grows in poor soil in disturbed sites east of the Rocky Mountains from Wyoming to Texas.

Coneflower   *Rudbeckia*

Coneflowers are tall, showy plants that have cylindrical centers of disk flowers. Depending on the species, yellow ray flowers may or may not be present. Coneflowers grow up to 40 inches tall and have small, alternate stem leaves and large basal leaves. We described two of the three species that occur in Wyoming.

Coneflowers grow in wet to moist, sunny soils in the plains, steppe, foothills, and montane zones.

Cutleaf coneflower (*Rudbeckia laciniata*) has a tall, branched stem with yellow ray flowers and a prominent cone of yellow disk flowers. The leaves are deeply pinnately divided into pointed lobes. It blooms in July and August. Found in the plains, steppe, and foothills, cutleaf coneflower is widespread in the Great Plains west to Montana, Utah, and Arizona.

Western rayless coneflower (*Rudbeckia occidentalis*) has no ray flowers, only a cylindrical cone of purple disk flowers. The cone grows up to $2^{1}/_{2}$ inches tall as the flower heads mature. Leaves are oval with prominent teeth. It blooms from June to August and grows along streambanks in thickets and open woods in the foothills and montane zones from western Wyoming to California, Nevada, and Utah.

Golden Curlyhead
Pyrrocoma crocea

Upright Prairie Coneflower
Ratibida columnifera

Cutleaf Coneflower
Rudbeckia laciniata

Western Rayless Coneflower
Rudbeckia occidentalis

Groundsel   *Senecio*

Species of the *Senecio* genus have showy yellow flower heads and basal leaves or leaves that occur along branched stems. Depending on the species, leaves may be simple, toothed, or divided. Flower heads have both ray and disk flowers and occur singly or in branched, flat-topped clusters. They have a ragged look since the ray flowers are spread unevenly around the disk flowers. The bracts surrounding the base of the flower head usually have black tips. An alkaloid produced by some species may cause liver damage in livestock. Thirty-two species occur in Wyoming.

Groundsels grow in various habitats in dry to moist soils in all vegetation zones.

Cutleaf groundsel *(Senecio eremophilus)* has coarsely toothed, lobed leaves with stems that grow up to 20 inches tall. It blooms in July and August and grows in gravelly soils along roadsides, in ditches, and in streambeds in the montane zone. It is widespread in western North America.

Lambstongue groundsel *(Senecio integerrimus)* has large, oval to elliptical, entire leaves with loose, cobweblike hair. It grows 18 inches tall. Quite common, it blooms in June, July, and August. Lambstongue groundsel favors undisturbed prairie and damp grassy soils. It grows in the plains, steppe, and foothills from southern British Columbia, Alberta, and Saskatchewan to Nevada, Utah, and New Mexico.

Arrowleaf groundsel *(Senecio triangularis)* is a tall, leafy plant that grows up to 5 feet tall. The leaves are triangular and have sharp teeth along their margins. It blooms in July and August and grows in moist or wet soils, usually in shade, in the foothills, montane, subalpine, and alpine zones throughout western North America.

Top left: Cutleaf Groundsel
Senecio eremophilus

Top right: Lambstongue
Groundsel
Senecio integerrimus

Bottom: Arrowleaf
Groundsel
Senecio triangularis

Goldenrod *Solidago*

These wildflowers are upright plants with densely leafy stems. Leaves are simple and bright green and have sharp teeth on their margins. Small flower heads have numerous tiny, gold ray flowers and gold disk flowers. The flower heads form crowded clusters on the tops of the stems. Goldenrods have been used in herbal medicines to heal wounds and stop bleeding. Thirteen species occur in Wyoming.

Goldenrods grow in moist places in all vegetation zones.

Canada goldenrod *(Solidago canadensis)* has triangular-shaped flower clusters and very leafy stems that may grow up to 5 feet tall. Lance-shaped leaves grow up to 4 inches long. Canada goldenrod is the state flower of Nebraska. It blooms from July to September and can be found at lower elevations along streams and in thickets in the plains, steppe, and foothills throughout the United States and Canada.

Northern goldenrod *(Solidago multiradiata)* has a large number of basal leaves and a few stem leaves on a narrowly branched stem. Leaves are narrow, spoon shaped, and grow up to 4 inches long. The plant grows 12 to 20 inches tall and has golden yellow flower heads in rounded terminal clusters. Northern goldenrod blooms in July and August. It can be found in the montane and subalpine zones and is widespread in western North America.

Stemless Goldenweed *Stenotus acaulis*

This wildflower grows in mats of shiny, elliptical basal leaves that have entire margins. The solitary flower heads have eight to ten entire, yellowish orange ray flowers on stalks that grow up to 6 inches tall. Stemless goldenweed was formerly named *Haplopappus acaulis*. Two *Stenotus* species occur in Wyoming.

Stemless goldenweed blooms from May to July and grows in dry, rocky soils in the steppe, foothills, montane, subalpine, and alpine zones. It occurs west of the Great Plains from southern British Columbia and Alberta to Colorado and Arizona.

Canada Goldenrod
Solidago canadensis

Northern Goldenrod
Solidago multiradiata

Stemless Goldenweed   *Stenotus acaulis*

Leafy Aster   *Symphyotrichum foliaceum*

This aptly named wildflower grows 20 inches tall and has very leafy stems and daisylike flower heads. The alternate, elliptical leaves grow 2 to 5 inches long. The flower heads are composed of gold disk flowers and fifteen to sixty purple ray flowers. Eighteen species in this genus occur in Wyoming; many were previously in the genus *Aster*.

Formerly named *Aster foliaceus*, leafy aster blooms in early August, grows in moist areas in the montane, subalpine, and alpine zones in the high mountains, and is widespread in western North America.

Stemless Sunflower   *Tetraneuris acaulis*

Stemless sunflower, also called *butte marigold*, has entire, narrow to elliptical, hairy basal leaves. The solitary flower heads, up to $1^{1}/_{4}$ inches broad, occur on stalks that grow up to 6 inches tall. They have gold ray flowers that are notched into three lobes at the tip, and centers of gold disk flowers. This wildflower was formerly called *Hymenoxys acaulis*. Two *Tetraneuris* species occur in Wyoming.

Stemless sunflower blooms in May and June. It grows in dry soil in the foothills, montane, subalpine, and alpine zones throughout western North America.

Townsendia   *Townsendia*

Most of these wildflowers are stemless, cushionlike, mat forming, and only grow a few inches tall. The hairy basal leaves are simple and have entire margins. Single, white to purple flower heads have smooth, evenly spaced ray flowers and golden yellow disk flowers. There are fourteen *Townsendia* species in Wyoming.

Townsendias bloom early in spring, in April and May, and are sometimes called *Easter daisies*. They grow in dry, sunny, rocky areas in all vegetation zones.

The flower heads of **Hooker's townsendia *(Townsendia hookeri)*** grow nestled among the basal leaves that are taller than the flowers. The flower heads, which occur singly or in clusters arising directly from the basal leaves, have fifteen to thirty white ray flowers with a yellow center of disk flowers. Hooker's townsendia grows in dry, open soils in the steppe and foothills zones. It occurs from southern Alberta and Saskatchewan to western South Dakota, Colorado, and eastern Utah.

Hoary townsendia *(Townsendia incana)* has narrow leaves covered with white hair, hairy stems, and whitish to pale pink ray flowers. Flower heads grow on the tips of branched stems. It grows in sandy soil in the steppe and foothills zones from Wyoming and western Colorado to New Mexico and Utah.

Leafy Aster
Symphyotrichum foliaceum

Stemless Sunflower
Tetraneuris acaulis

Hooker's Townsendia
Townsendia hookeri

Hoary Townsendia
Townsendia incana

Showy Goldeneye   *Viguiera multiflora*

Showy goldeneye has leafy, erect stems with open branches. It may grow up to 36 inches tall. The opposite leaves have entire margins and are lance shaped. The showy, bright yellow flower heads, up to 1½ inches across, have ten to fourteen ray flowers and gold disk flowers on a rounded center. This is the only *Viguiera* species in Wyoming.

Showy goldeneye blooms from July to September and grows in dry, sunny areas of the foothills, montane, and subalpine zones from southwestern Montana and eastern Idaho to New Mexico and Nevada.

Mule's Ears   *Wyethia*

These robust, perennial plants have large, yellow flower heads composed of ray and disk flowers. Leaves are simple, alternate, and elliptical. Plants grow 12 to 24 inches tall. This genus was named in honor of Nathaniel Wyeth who, in 1833, was the first botanist to collect plants in Wyoming. Three *Wyethia* species occur in Wyoming.

These plants grow in dry or moist soils in the steppe, foothills, and montane zones.

Mule's ears *(Wyethia amplexicaulis)* has smooth, green, shiny, varnished leaves that are elliptical and have a wide base; they are shaped like a mule's ears. Flower heads are up to 3 inches across and have thirteen to twenty-two yellow ray flowers. Branched stems have a large flower head at the top and a few smaller flower heads on side branches. Mule's ears bloom in May and June and grow in moist soils in the foothills and montane zones mostly west of the Continental Divide from Washington to Montana south to Utah and central Colorado.

Whitestem sunflower *(Wyethia scabra)* is a rough, stiff plant with hairy, narrow to lance-shaped leaves and hairy white stems. The flower heads have ten to eighteen ray flowers and grow up to 2½ inches across. Whitestem sunflower blooms from May to August and grows in dry, sandy soils in steppe. It occurs from central Wyoming and Utah to New Mexico and Arizona.

Showy Goldeneye   *Viguiera multiflora*

Mule's Ears   *Wyethia amplexicaulis*

Whitestem Sunflower   *Wyethia scabra*

Woody Aster *Xylorhiza glabriuscula*

Found in dry, sagebrush steppe, woody aster grows on soils that contain selenium. This plant is toxic to grazing animals since it concentrates the mineral in its tissues. It has unbranched, stiff stems that grow up to 12 inches tall and bright green, elliptical leaves. Leaves have fine teeth and sharply pointed, spiny tips. The flower heads have white ray flowers and a center of yellow disk flowers. The flower heads have a slightly ragged appearance because the ray flowers are attached unevenly around the disk flowers. This is the only *Xylorhiza* species in Wyoming.

Woody aster blooms in May and grows in dry, clay soils in the steppe in Wyoming, Montana, South Dakota, Colorado, and Utah.

VALERIAN FAMILY Valerianaceae

The valerian family is comprised of herbs that have a strong odor and opposite leaves. The flowers have five very narrow sepals, five united petals with five lobes, and three stamens. The flowers are small and clustered on tall stems. The family has three hundred species distributed worldwide, mostly in the cooler parts of the Northern Hemisphere.

Western Valerian *Valeriana occidentalis*

Western valerian has tall, leafy stems that grow 12 to 36 inches tall. Somewhat fleshy, the pinnately lobed, opposite leaves have rounded, egg-shaped leaflets. The tiny flowers have five united, white petals. They are grouped in compact, half-rounded flower clusters that are held upright on leafy stems. Valerian has long been used in herbal medicine as a sedative. When bruised or dried, these plants give off an objectionable odor and are sometimes known by the common name *stinky socks*. Five *Valeriana* species occur in Wyoming.

Western valerian flowers from May to July and grows in moist to wet soils in shade along streams and in open meadows in the foothills, montane, subalpine, and alpine zones from Idaho, Montana, and Wyoming into Colorado and Utah.

Woody Aster *Xylorhiza glabriuscula*

Western Valerian *Valeriana occidentalis*

VIOLET FAMILY Violaceae

The violet family is composed of perennial or annual herbs that have simple, basal and alternate leaves. Dainty, irregular flowers have five sepals, five separate petals, and five stamens. Six hundred species occur worldwide. Many, such as the pansy and Johnny-jump-up (*Viola* species), are garden favorites or are used as herbal remedies.

Violet *Viola*

Growing in low, rounded clumps, violets are known for their beautiful flowers. The blossoms have five petals: two upper ones and three lower ones; the central lower petal is slightly larger than the others. The leaves are lance shaped or heart shaped. Both leaves and flowers are sometimes eaten as greens or made into tea. Fourteen *Viola* species grow in Wyoming.

Violets grow in dry or moist sites in all vegetation zones.

Hook violet *(Viola adunca)* has violet to blue flowers that have dark purple lines on the lower petals. Leaves are mostly basal and the plant grows up to 4 inches tall. You can find it in bloom in late May in the foothills and as late as July in the alpine zone. It grows in open meadows and woods in all vegetation zones and is widespread across western North America.

Canada violet *(Viola canadensis)* has white flowers that are tinged with dark violet veins. It has leafy stems, round and heart-shaped leaves, and it grows 4 to 16 inches tall. Look for it blooming in June in moist, wooded thickets and mature forests in the foothills and montane zones. It is widespread in western North America.

Yellow violet *(Viola nuttallii)* has yellow flowers with faint purple veins. The elliptical leaves are longer than they are wide. It grows 2 to 4 inches tall. This violet is common in steppe, and it blooms in early May at the same time as shooting star (*Dodecatheon* species) and phlox (*Phlox* species). It occurs in all vegetation zones from southern British Columbia and Alberta to New Mexico.

Hook Violet
Viola adunca

Canada Violet
Viola canadensis

Yellow Violet
Viola nuttallii

WATERLEAF FAMILY   Hydrophyllaceae

The waterleaf family, most commonly found in the dry habitats of the western United States, includes three hundred species. The plants are usually covered with rough hair, and the flowers grow in tightly coiled clusters. Flowers have five united sepals, five united petals, and five stamens that usually protrude beyond the petals.

Ballhead Waterleaf *Hydrophyllum capitatum*

Ballhead waterleaf has alternate, pinnately compound leaves with five to seven rounded leaflets. The short, 2- to 8-inch flower stalks barely rise above the leaves. The light-violet flowers occur in compact, coiled, globe-shaped clusters and have stamens that extend beyond the petals. Two *Hydrophyllum* species grow in Wyoming.

Ballhead waterleaf usually blooms in May and June. It is common on gravelly slopes and glacial moraines in the foothills, montane, and subalpine zones from southern British Columbia and Alberta to Colorado, Utah, and Nevada.

Phacelia *Phacelia*

These plants have unbranched stems and grow 4 to 16 inches tall. The stems and leaves are covered with silky, silvery hair. The funnel-shaped flowers, with five united petals, have stamens that protrude beyond the petals, giving the flowers a fuzzy appearance. Eighteen *Phacelia* species occur in Wyoming.

They grow in dry, rocky sites, often along roadsides, in all vegetation zones.

Silver-leaved scorpionweed (*Phacelia hastata*) has off-white to light-lavender flowers that grow in compact clusters composed of coiled side clusters. The alternate leaves are elliptical and entire. It is called scorpionweed because the flower clusters are coiled when young and uncoil as the flowers open, resembling a scorpion's tail. Silver-leaved scorpionweed blooms in June and July and is found in all vegetation zones from southern British Columbia and Alberta to Colorado.

Silky phacelia (*Phacelia sericea*) has hairy leaves that are deeply pinnately divided into pointed lobes. The flowers are purple with purple and yellow stamens; the stamens extend beyond the petals and make the flower clusters look like bottlebrushes. It blooms in May and June and can usually be seen on roadsides and along trails in the foothills, montane, subalpine, and alpine zones from southern British Columbia and Alberta to Colorado, Utah, and Nevada.

Ballhead Waterleaf *Hydrophyllum capitatum*

Silver-Leaved Scorpionweed
Phacelia hastata

Silky Phacelia
Phacelia sericea

WATER-LILY FAMILY   Nymphaceae

The water-lily family is composed of ninety species of aquatic perennials with large leaves and brightly colored flowers. They occur in temperate and tropical waters worldwide. Flowers have seven to nine showy sepals, ten to twenty small petals, and many stamens.

Rocky Mountain Pondlily   *Nuphar polysepalum*
This aquatic plant grows below water level and has large, floating leaves. The leaves are round to heart shaped, leathery, shiny, and grow 4 to 12 inches long. The flowers have up to nine showy, waxy, yellow sepals, and ten to twenty tiny petals hidden behind stamens. The cup-shaped blossom is 3 to 5 inches across. The flowers are held above the leaves on a smooth naked stem. This is the only *Nuphar* species in Wyoming.

Rocky Mountain pondlily blooms in July and grows in the shallow, quiet water of lakes and ponds in the plains, foothills, and montane zones throughout western North America.

WATER MILFOIL FAMILY   Haloragaceae

The aquatic plants of this family are distributed on all continents. Only a handful of the one hundred species of this family occur in the United States. Tiny flowers have four sepals, four petals, and eight stamens.

Water Milfoil   *Myriophyllum sibericum*
Only the tips of the red-stemmed branches and flower stalks of these submerged, aquatic plants grow above water. Leaves are finely dissected into hairlike divisions and are grouped in whorls along the stem. Flowers have two to four inconspicuous, greenish petals and are also grouped in whorls along the elongated stems. This wildflower, often overlooked by humans, provides seeds for waterfowl. Three *Myriophyllum* species occur in Wyoming.

Water milfoil blooms in July and August and occurs in still or slow-moving water in the plains, foothills, and montane zones. It is widespread in western North America.

WATER-PLANTAIN FAMILY   Alismataceae

The water-plantain family has about seventy species that occur in the warm and temperate zones of the Northern Hemisphere. The aquatic plants have flowers with three sepals, three petals, and six stamens.

Arrowhead   *Sagittaria cuneata*
Arrowhead, named for its arrowhead-shaped leaves, is aquatic and oozes milky juice when cut. The flowers have three white, round petals that are about 1 inch across. They occur in clusters of three and are held above the water's surface

Rocky Mountain Pondlily *Nuphar polysepalum*

Water Milfoil *Myriophyllum sibericum*

Arrowhead *Sagittaria cuneata*

by a stem. The tuberlike roots and leaves of this plant provide food for ducks and muskrats. Two *Sagittaria* species occur in Wyoming.

Arrowhead blooms from June to September and grows along sandy shores and in the mudflats of ponds and lakes in the plains, steppe, foothills, and montane zones from southern British Columbia, Alberta, and Saskatchewan to California and New Mexico.

SELECTED REFERENCES

Barkley, T. M., ed. 1991. *Flora of the Great Plains.* Lawrence, Kans.: University of Kansas Press.

Cronquist, A., A. Holmgren, N. Holmgren, J. Reveal. 1972. *Intermountain Flora: Vascular Plants of the Intemountain West, U.S.A.,* vols. 1, 3, 4–6. Bronx, N.Y.: The New York Botanical Garden.

Dorn, Robert D. 2001. *Vascular Plants of Wyoming,* 3rd ed. Cheyenne, Wyo.: Mountain West Publishing. Distributed By Rocky Mountain Herbarium, University of Wyoming, Laramie.

Evans, Howard E. 1993. *Pioneer Naturalists: The Discovery and Naming of North American Plants and Animals.* N.Y.: Henry Holt and Co.

Porter, C. L. 1959. *Taxonomy of Flowering Plants.* San Francisco, Calif.: W. H. Freeman and Co.

Scott, Richard W. 1995. *The Alpine Flora of the Rocky Mountains,* vol. 1, *The Middle Rockies.* Salt Lake City, Utah: University of Utah Press.

Tilford, Gregory L. 1997. *Edible and Medicinal Plants of the West.* Missoula, Mont.: Mountain Press Publishing Co.

Whitson, Tom D., ed. 1992. *Weeds of the West.* Laramie: Western Society of Weed Science and University of Wyoming.

NATIVE PLANT SOCIETIES

Colorado Native Plant Society, P.O. Box 200, Fort Collins, CO 80522-0200

Great Plains Native Plant Society, P.O. Box 461, Hot Springs, SD 57747-0461

Idaho Native Plant Society, P.O. Box 9451, Boise, ID 83707-3451

Montana Native Plant Society, P.O. Box 8783, Missoula, MT 59807-8783

Utah Native Plant Society, P.O. Box 520041, Salt Lake City, UT 84152-0041

Wyoming Native Plant Society, P.O. Box 3452, 1604 Grand Avenue, Laramie, WY 82071

INDEX AND CHECKLIST

ABOUT THE AUTHORS

Diantha States was born and raised on the plains of eastern North Dakota. Influenced by her grandmother who taught her bird and wildflower identification, she developed a love of the outdoors. She studied botany and received a bachelor's degree from North Dakota State University and a master's degree in botany and plant ecology from Oregon State University. She lives in Lander, Wyoming, with her husband, Jack.

A native of Wyoming, **Jack States** was raised in a beekeeping family in Saratoga. He received a bachelor's degree in education and a master's degree in botany from the University of Wyoming and worked as a recreation specialist for the U.S. Forest Service and as a seasonal ranger in Grand Teton National Park while in school. After earning a doctorate in botany from the University of Alberta, Jack taught for twenty-five years at Northern Arizona University at Flagstaff before retiring in 1995.